TURN NINE EXECUTE

RICHARD MAX BOSSHARDT

outskirts
press

I dedicate my book to my wife of 49 years, JOAN, who shared experiences while I served on the U.S.S Goodrich DDR-831.

Acknowledgments

I wish to acknowledge the following persons who either provided their own experiences or helped me put this book together.

Leo J. Chamberlain LT (jg)

Charles Henry LT (jg)

Robert Perry LT (jg)

Richard Beyers RD 3

John Martucci MM 3

Edward J. Frketic

LWW Writers, Lew Istre, President, & members

Durinda Kelley Author

Table of Contents

CHAPTER 1

The Time Had
Finally Come

I drove my old college Dodge coupe from my home in Swarthmore, Pennsylvania, picked up Henry Ver Valen in Philadelphia, and went up Old Route 1 to Newport, Rhode Island, to deliver Henry to his assigned DE. Henry and I had shared Engineering School and Varsity lacrosse at Cornell, as well as Midshipman cruises together.

Then I drove on to Boston, at that time a grueling 12-hour trip, and had to find the Boston Naval Shipyard at night. It was a struggle finding my way in. I made it just before midnight to save a day of leave. Of course, by then my anxiety meter was running at full tilt.

The U.S.S. *Goodrich*, to which I was assigned, was in dry dock during a three-month major overhaul. My vision of presenting myself to a majestic and sleek destroyer along-side a pier, with colors flying, was totally shattered. There was no one at the quarterdeck to whom I could present myself, salute and request permission to come on board.

Instead, it was the opening scene of *The Caine Mutiny* all over again: temporary shipyard lights casting ominous shadows across a deck littered with scrap metal, welding lines, and not one crew member.

I made my way down to the mess deck and found one mate of the watch who was watching TV. He volunteered to rouse the CDO out of forward officers' quarters, where he was asleep. A sleepy LT (jg) stumbled out and introduced himself as Bob Bryant. He suggested it was too late to make my way back to the BOQ (Bachelor Officers' Quarters) and get a bunk, so he put me in a bunk loaded with six mattresses stowed there. My head was just under the overhead. Somehow, I managed to get some sleep mixed with what seemed like hours of rest-lessness contemplating my horrible new situation.

At 07:00 the next morning, the shipyard workers start-ed with their riveting hammers right over my head and shocked the shit out of me. Hastily, I shaved with cold water, put on my spanking new summer Ensign's uni-form, stumbled out on deck, tripping over welding lines everywhere, (exactly as in the movie *The Caine Mutiny*) and made my way onto the dock where the crew stood muster. I found the Engineering Department, with 90 scruffy dungaree-clad sailors and the Chief Engineer, LT Craig Smith. He was a pissed off reservist, called back to active duty, and going crazy with all the shipyard liaison work. He looked at the crew and said, "Men, this is your new division officer, Mr. Bosshardt." He then turned to me and said, "Take over!" and walked off.

It was almost life's darkest moment. I didn't have a clue. I weakly said "Dismissed." Later that morning, I had to go to the Boston Naval Recruiting Station in Chelsea for a physical. Coming out, still in my new uniform, a drunk stumbled up to me and said, "I hate you rotten officers!" At that point, I thought, "GOOD GOD, WHAT AM I DOING IN THIS DAMNED NAVY?" I could easily have deserted right then and there.

It was Ensign Leo Chamberlain, whom I caught up with later at the ship's office in the Navy Yard, who restored my confidence. He was a friend indeed, as were Ezra Bixby and Fred Dent, each of whom was a seasoned Lieutenant Junior Grade."

Four midshipmen in Panama: Leo on the left and I am on the right.

CHAPTER 2

About Midshipman Days

Leo Chamberlain had been very instrumental in helping me get started as a new ensign. Leo came from a family in New York. His father was Chief Engineer at CBS. Leo's brother, Al, studied psychology. Leo was an intense, dedicated person, and like me, studied electrical engineering. Yet under the surface lurked a fantastic sense of humor, which, despite a straight face, could burst out at any time. Because the Engineering College at Cornell University required five years to obtain a Bachelor's degree, it happened that Leo was one year ahead of me in electrical engineering, but we shared the same four years as NROTC Midshipmen.

One year, Leo came back to the dormitory from the library and told us he had noticed a charming looking coed. We asked her name, and other details, but for weeks Leo did not have the nerve to go over and speak to her.

Finally, he found an excuse to approach her and managed to arrange a date. Her name was Leah Shumaker; she was petite and extremely attractive. To make a long story short, Leo and Leah eloped while they were still at Cornell, and he had to keep this secret from the Navy as it was not permitted to be married until you have been commissioned.

In the ensuing years at Cornell, we had to go eight to ten weeks training cruise each summer on ships in the U.S. Navy.

There were always six or eight of us from Cornell who traveled together. Included were Leo, Henry Ver Valen, Vinnie Crane, and Walt Bortko.

The first summer in 1949, we rode the California Zephyr out to the West Coast, arriving several days early so we could visit San Francisco. After checking into the YMCA, we stepped out on the street to make our way into the city. A gentleman rushed up to us and said he was the Mayor of San Francisco, and they were forming a parade around the corner. He needed us, in uniform, each to escort a debutante lady in a convertible and take part in the parade. It was all true, and we couldn't believe our eyes. In the very first hours of our arrival in San Francisco, we were riding up Market Street in convertibles with thousands of people lining the streets! At the head of the parade were Roy Rogers and Dale Evans. The next day we purchased several newspapers with pictures of the parade and sent them home to our families.

The next day, the scene had changed radically. We checked in on Goat Island, received sailors' uniforms to wear on the ship, had our heads shaved clean, and reported on board the USS Toledo, a heavy cruiser.

Our training was thorough and rigorous, and we had to assume all operating stations just like the crew. A training exercise with a battalion of US Marines, who were to make an amphibious landing on Catalina Island, was canceled because they had been sent directly to South Korea. The Korean War was well in progress.l

We landed in Balboa, on the Pacific side of the Panama Canal. Our group of six midshipmen prepared to go ashore on liberty, but we were a little bit unnerved when the Chief Pharmacist Mate handed out kits for each of us containing sulfa-thiosol ointment tubes, condoms, and other medicaments to protect us from VD. We were glad that one of our group, Walt Bortko, was with us. He was a barrel chested, tough looking guy from Brooklyn. So we hired a taxi and rode out into the jungle to a plantation house, to see the famous "exhibition."

We were escorted upstairs to a large bedroom in the plantation house. Two very black middle-aged and over-weight Panamanian women got up on the king-sized bed with very few clothes on. We were all sitting on chairs around the bed to watch the event. I think they engaged each other in every possible way that two women can in-dulge themselves sexually. Far from being sexually aroused watching them, the sight of these rather ugly women, the fear of catching a venereal disease, and being so remotely located in an isolated part of the jungle, really turned us off. As we took our leave, we were amazed and shocked that Walt wanted us to wait while he had intercourse in private with one of the women.

We did return to the ship unscathed. The next day, the scene changed abruptly, as we were invited to go in dress blues to a lovely country club and attend a dance at the sponsorship of the local diplomatic corps. I became quite thrilled to meet and dance with a lovely young lady, who, although having very dark skin, had very fine features. She was the daughter of an ambassador.

The ship had an open house for visitors the next day, and I invited the young lady to come see me on board for a tour. I became further embarrassed as many of the crewmembers observed her walking along the pier and up the gangway to meet me. However, she must have really impressed me because I still remember her telephone number today as dos ocha ocha ocha bay (2888 B). Needless to say, we exchanged letters.

The midshipman cruise concluded with a stopover by the USS Toledo at the Galapagos Islands directly on the equator. While at anchor for 24 hours, those of us who had never crossed the equator and were known as "pollywogs" suffered a terrible initiation. Many of the ships crew had crossed the equator previously and numbered about 600 men and were able to organize and herd the other 900 of us who had never crossed through the torture. First, we crawled across the deck while some 30 sailors equipped with long canvas tubes stuffed with rags and dipped in salt water whacked us across our bottoms. We then sat on deck as they cooled off our stinging rear ends with cold seawater. The culmination of the all-day events was to mount a stage, with Davy Jones and Neptunus Rex holding court, kiss the Royal baby's belly (a chief petty officer with a large belly smeared with grease), then sit in a chair, which dumped us over backwards into a tank of slimy water. Every time we emerged we were asked, "What are you?" and we would scream "Pollywog!" After about the third or fourth dunking, it dawned on us that we had now become "shellbacks" and were released.

One of the most frightening aspects of the whole exercise was a group of five or ten pollywogs who thought, by their sheer numbers, that they could take over command of the ship. However, they were quickly rounded up, shoved into a large iron cage, which the ship's crane on the fantail then lowered over the side into the sea with two thirds of the cage submerged. The fear of sharks quickly subdued the renegades' enthusiasm to fight back!

Among all the diplomas and certificates that hung on my bulkhead, the large Shellback Certificate, signed by Neptunus Rex himself, is the most revered of all.

The Midshipman training summer in 1950 was an introduction to two types of naval operations. I rejoined my Cornell classmate, and fellow varsity lacrosse player, Henry VerValen. We had to travel a hot and torturous train ride from the Northeast through the southern states to Pensacola, Florida.

We certainly were highly impressed with the high level of training conducted by naval aviators. We had our opportunity to ride the centrifuge, get in a flight simulator, and experience the apparatus which taught Naval pilots what to do when ditching at sea, as this huge machine resembled a cockpit, into which the pilot was strapped, rode the steel rails into a swimming pool, turned over and submerged. Luckily, there were UDT men in the pool to help the poor bastards who could not get out of the cockpit.

We were sent out for a day on an aircraft carrier to observe six new pilots attempting their first landings on the carrier. It consisted of six landings, each next take-off following the previous landing immediately, and going around again to land. For the noon meal that day, we were able to sit with the pilots who completed their landings. Only three made it, and were drenched in sweat. The other three had to return to Pensacola. I think naval pilots earned their extra bonus pay.

The whole business of flight training was further impressed upon me when I went up with a pilot in an SNJ single-engine, two-seat training aircraft. One seat was behind the other. Below my seat all the mechanisms needed to steer this plane were exposed below my feet. Before we departed, the pilot instructed me to roll down the sleeves of my shirt and button the cuff. He told me that if I got airsick, I was to vomit up my shirt sleeve because, otherwise, it would take me hours to clean up all the mechanisms down in the bilge of the plane. Of course, soon after takeoff, he told me on the intercom to hold tight, and then immediately did a complete barrel roll over backwards. I don't even remember the several maneuvers he made after that, I was so close to vomiting that my total concentration was focused on keeping it down in my stomach.

Upon arrival at Pensacola, during our first liberty, Henry and I went into town to a used car lot and purchased the first car we ever owned. We paid $50 for a model A Ford whose front windshield could be raised up to get air circulation.

The gas gauge was broken so we used a ruler to stick into the gas tank periodically to find out how much fuel we still had left. But make no mistake; we were the cat's meows with the girls in town. At the end of our Pensacola session, we took the Ford back to the same used car lot and sold it back for $50.

Then, it was the hot, horrible train ride again through the South, frequently stopping for no reason, and nothing to drink. Eventually, we arrived at Little Creek, Virginia, near Norfolk, for amphibious landing training. This was the worst. I remember putting on full combat gear, with weapons and helmets and embarking in a crowded LST. The idea was to land on a beach and storm ashore like

Marine combat troops. However, the one sailor on board who was the Coxswain must have surmised that this was his only chance to stick it to future officers. Some 15 yards off the beach, he stopped the LST and, when we jumped out, we were in some five to six feet of seawater with the waves rolling by. Somehow, with all our gear on and soaking wet, we made our way to the beach and had to crawl up the beach picking up half the sand that was there. Horrible!

The summer of 1951, our last summer cruise, was much improved. We were on the heavy cruiser USS Newport News and operated from the East Coast to Halifax, Canada, then to Boston, Guantánamo Bay, and back to New York. As first-class midshipmen, we felt ourselves thoroughly trained and experienced in all naval operation matters. We had no inkling of the next phase when we were to report on our assigned ships. As very green ensigns, we experienced our first confrontations taking charge of seasoned sailors.

CHAPTER 3

Another Shock

The first few months during the shipyard overhaul seemed to pass very quickly. In the first days, Leo was helpful in introducing me to the ship's other officers. I initially presented myself to LCDR Hemmingson, who was the executive officer and who took care of all administrative and personnel matters.

Of course, with my degree in electrical engineering and an open billet in the engineering department, it was obvious that I should be assigned to that department as the fourth officer, with the title and function of Electrical Officer. Senior to me were LT (jg) Fred Dent, Damage Control Officer, and LT (jg) Shapiro, Main Propulsion Assistant, all of us reporting to LT Craig Smith, Chief Engineer. Craig seemed to be the most hassled and busy officer of all, because he was the principal liaison between the shipyard workers and our ship's organization.

I also had a brief introduction to our Captain (Commanding Officer), CDR Bob Hayler. He was a Naval Academy graduate, and his father had been an Admiral. As Captain of the Goodrich, CDR Hayler had a fantastic reputation as an excellent ship handler and always maintained a very cool composure on the bridge no matter what the circumstances might be. More about that later from the experience of Leo Chamberlain.

As a junior officer in the engineering department, I also had the responsibility of being the division officer and directly concerned with the personnel needs of some 90 sailors in the engineering department.

Major changes were being made to the superstructure since the Goodrich had been transformed from a Sumner class destroyer (DD) into a radar picket ship (DDR). 40 mm gun mounts were replaced by the newer three inch 50 caliber gun mounts as our secondary armament; torpedoes were replaced, and there were many additions topside of new radar.

To my recollection, no new "inclining experiment" was performed. This is performed in dry dock to newly constructed ships. It is a confirmation of the Naval architects' calculations of the location of the center of gravity of the ship. For a surface ship, the center of gravity is above the center of buoyancy, about which a ship rolls in the water. That is why a surface ship making a turn leans outboard to the turn. In other words, the center of gravity acts as a lever arm over the center of buoyancy. On the other hand, submarines and airplanes, have the opposite effect because the center of gravity is below the center of buoyancy, and these vessels lean inward when making a turn. Because a submarine behaves like a ship when on the surface, there is a moment when it is submerging that the center of gravity passes through the center of buoyancy at which point the submarine has no stability against rolling.

The inclining experiment consists of adding known weights at measured distances from the centerline as the ship floats in the dry dock filled with water, and the angles of heel are thus plotted. A calculation can then be made as to the maximum angle of heel a ship can withstand and still maintain a righting arm to bring the ship back to its vertical position after a wave has caused it to roll to one side. The Goodrich had a design and maximum role capability of 76°. But the changes in topside structure and equipment, such as the gun mounts and radars located higher up, caused some considerable question later as to how much of a roll the ship could take without rolling over completely.

Sometime later in the summer, when I had become much more acclimated to the situation and my duties, Craig Smith finished his second tour of duty and was discharged. Al Schapiro became Chief Engineer, and I moved up to Main Propulsion Assistant. We acquired another more junior officer, Dave Wiley, and Fred Dent stayed on board as damage Control Officer.

The day finally came in early September when we could leave the shipyard in Boston. By this time CDR Tom Keegan had arrived and took over as Captain of the Goodrich, relieving CDR Hayler. Tom Keegan was a very personable officer and more approachable. He had come from the submarine service but had never commanded a destroyer or any other surface ship. We were ordered to proceed to Newport, Rhode Island, our homeport, and shortly thereafter departed for a brief visit to San Juan, Puerto Rico, before ending up at Guantanamo Bay, Cuba. There we would conduct our annual two-week refresher training.

Unfortunately, about this time, a major hurricane was advancing off and up the East Coast of the United States. In those days, there were no satellites or hurricane chasing aircraft to give exact positions as to the center of the hurricane. We only received a telex message every four hours of the approximate position of the storm. As we departed for San Juan, Captain Keegan decided that hurricane Carol was far enough offshore that he could take the Goodrich southwards between Cape Hatteras, North Carolina, and the approximate center of the storm to the eastward and therefore miss the brunt of the storm as it moved northwards. But the size of hurricane Carol was monstrous! It had a diameter of 800 miles and the eye of the storm was about 30 miles in diameter. Thus there was no possible way for the Goodrich to avoid direct entry into the hurricane in its western half, whose winds and waves were already reaching the coast. Because a hurricane in the northern hemisphere has a northward motion, the circulating winds of the hurricane, which rotate counter clockwise, are increased on the eastern half of the storm (dangerous semicircle) and decreased on the western half of the storm (safe semicircle) by the forward motion. So we had some luck in entering the western portion. However, the difference was hardly discernible.

In no time at all we were entering waves of 30 to 40 feet, from trough to crest. The height of our bridge was only 27 feet. At that point, we could no longer select our course but were forced to steer a course 45° to the waves. Had we steamed parallel to the waves, we surely would have rolled over, and if we steamed directly into the waves the ship would have been broken into two or three sections. The ship made very slow progress, and all four motions of a ship came into play simultaneously: rolling, pitching, yawing, and heaving. Standing on the bridge, one would look up at the approaching crest of the next wave. Then suddenly, the ship seemed to ride up with the bow in the air and heeling over at a crazy angle until the wave passed below us. It seemed that we hung in this position for a matter of seconds until the stern came out of the water and rolled to the opposite side and plunged bow first into the next trough. It was truly frightening. All hatches on the main deck had to remain closed, as the main deck was mostly underwater. The aluminum deck in the pilot house was wet and slick, and, in one instance, I slid towards the open door at the starboard side of the pilothouse. I grabbed the overhead transom, and my feet swung up over the combing at the side of the bridge to the point where I felt as if I would fall overboard. Our inclinometer was measuring a maximum roll angle of 54 degrees.

Three days in that storm seemed like eternity because we were awake most of the night. In order to sleep, one had to wedge the mattress to one side of the bunk's iron railing, with the body wedged between the mattress and the railing, and a belt fastened over your body to keep from rolling out. All drawers were pulled out and stacked on the deck and all chairs turned over. To add more misery to the situation, the ship creaked and groaned all night long as it twisted through the waves.

On one occasion, when I was junior officer of the deck on watch at night, a report came up that the motor whaleboat had broken loose of its stanchions and was swinging wildly on the davits, banging into various things. I was ordered to go back with several boatswains' mates to try to secure the motor whaleboat. We were standing on the 01 deck (one deck above the main deck) and waves were rolling knee deep across the deck. One boatswain's mate, who was particularly brave, volunteered to go down on the main deck and throw a line over the motor whaleboat so that we could secure it. We tied a safety line around him, and it seemed he was more underwater on the main deck than not. But he managed to get a line around the middle of the whaleboat, which we then could tighten with an electric winch and thus secure the motor whaleboat from swinging.

On the second day we passed through the eye of the storm, where it was sunny and calm with waves no larger than three feet. But, of course, we then had to traverse the circular winds again through mountains of waves in a southerly direction to exit the storm.

Everyone had to be extremely careful in walking about the ship. If a man had gone overboard, there was no way in hell we could turn the ship around to save him.

Eating was a real chore, with chairs being tied to the table and one's elbows spread across the table to keep from sliding to port or starboard, and holding a glass of milk in one hand and a sandwich in the other. Everyone, including the salty most seasoned boatswain's mate, felt ill, but I know of no one who actually got seasick to the point of vomiting. I think the three thumb rules to keep from getting seasick saved us all: Keep a full stomach. All day we would carry a box of saltine crackers around and constantly eat some; Stay in the fresh air as much as possible; Always keep our eyes focused far away, on the horizon, and never look directly down at the wild water.

The only other exception was in the main control engine room. Standing on the upper platform one was located exactly at the center of buoyancy of the ship. At this point one suffered very little motion.

Eventually, on the third day, the skies cleared, the waves

diminished, and we approached the harbor of San Juan. In spite of the distance from the main storm, there were still eight foot waves completely engulfing the channel buoys.

Hurricane Carol was certainly the most awesome experience of my whole life.

CHAPTER 4

A False Reputation

After a brief stop in San Juan, Puerto Rico, we reached our destination, Guantánamo Bay, Cuba.

I must take note of the fact that, today, the name and location evoke strong emotions and totally false impressions among the vast majority of Americans. In actual fact, for more than 100 years, and long before the media talked about terrorist prisoners at Guantánamo, the U.S. Navy created the ideal training facility there because virtually every day of the year has clear weather and warm temperatures. Permanent naval personnel are stationed there to support and conduct the annual retraining of every ship in the Atlantic Fleet. It is a system which produces excellent results when one considers that any given ship has a 50 percent turnover of its personnel every two years.

In 1900, the Cuban government and the U.S. Navy signed a 100-year lease for the territory of Guantánamo Bay, which lies on the easternmost end of the island of Cuba. It is an attractive place surrounding a large bay and a ring of mountains from which freshwater is collected from the occasional rainstorms. It is equipped with every imaginable training device and school, sports facilities, recreational facilities complete with an officers club and enlisted man's club in which drinks cost 10 cents each.

In the late 1950s, Fidel Castro started his communist revolution in the eastern mountains above Guantánamo. He tried to force the U.S. Navy out by shutting off the water supply from the mountains to the naval base. The U.S. Navy solved that problem with a clever move without firing a single shot. They simply fired all 400 Cuban workers at the base and told them that when the water was turned back on they could have their good paying jobs back again. It only took two days!

By the year 2000, when the lease was up, Castro was hard pressed for foreign currency. As a result, he continued the lease indefinitely. As far as I know it still goes on at the rate of only $4,000 per month.

Bruce Tharp recalls:

"As to ship handling itself, I think Capt. Keegan's problem lay in the fact that he came to the Goodrich from submarines, where his experience was with single screw vessels. He had not been involved in handling a twin-screw ship before. He took over while we were in the Boston Navy Yard in the summer of 1953. I recall he had a bit of trouble coming alongside the dock when we came back from our first sea trial. But what really stands out in my mind was what happened tying up at a dock in Guantanamo. I was on the bridge for some reason, perhaps as OOD for special sea detail, I forget. In summary, a strong offshore wind was blowing, and Keegan made several tries to get close enough to throw over a line, only to be blown back short of his goal each time. On one occasion, a message came up from the foc'sle asking for permission to use a line-throwing gun. He refused, obviously not wanting to suffer the ignominy of having that reflection on his ship handling. He made a final try that involved him stopping the engines too late, resulting in the ship ramming a sea wall."

Bruce described the annual visit to Guantanomo very concisely as follows:

"The Goodrich was in Guantanamo Bay for refresher training, having just completed a five-month overhaul in the Boston Navy Yard. These periods are scheduled to allow the crew to reach fighting trim, and become proficient once more in all aspects of the ship's mission after the long period of inactivity. The program at Gitmo involved steaming out each day for exercises in every aspect of the ship's operation, under the observation of personnel stationed at the base whose mission was to advise and monitor progress toward acceptable performance, advise regarding the nature of the retraining and, ultimately, certify the ship as ready to return to normal duty."

(end of Bruce's recollections).

For every ship going there for their annual two-week training, like the Goodrich, it was an intense and brutal affair. During the day, the ship would engage in tactical maneuvers such as attacks against submarines, shore bombardment, air attacks, etc. And then, after returning to the Bay to anchor, around five in the afternoon, we then had to begin doing the normal ship's work and maintenance. Not only that, but all night long we were on alert to fend off UDT attacks, whose frogmen swimmers also were there in training.

One of the few incidents recalled by a crew member was told by John Martucci:

"At the time when our ship, the *Goodrich*, was making its normal training cruise to Guantánamo, Cuba, a rather painful incident happened to me. As was customary in that hot climate, following a shower in the crew quarters, I wrapped a towel around myself and went back to my bunk, which was on the top level of a three-tier bunk. I stepped on the lower bunk and pushed my stomach over the rail of my own bunk, reaching for the opposite rail to pull myself up. Unfortunately, my towel became loose from my body and a stiff strand of hemp rope, used to stretch the canvas of the bunk, pierced and penetrated the head of my penis.

It was quite painful, and I wasn't able to remove the coarse fiber. Immediately, I went to the sick bay to get help from the Chief Medical Corpsman. He told me it required more delicate surgery than he was qualified to do; he sent me ashore to the Navy hospital at Guantánamo.

When I entered the outpatient waiting room, I was surprised to see about 15 or 20 people waiting, predominantly Navy wives. At that point, the medical corpsman came over to me with his clipboard and asked what my problem was. I became very embarrassed in front of all these ladies and whispered to him very softly that a fiber had penetrated the head of my penis. At that point, he said he couldn't hear me and would I speak louder. As if that wasn't embarrassing enough, I was called in and confronted by a female Navy nurse. Not only was she a female but a very tough lady who didn't use a gentle approach. As a preexam before my visit with the doctor, she took me behind an exam screen and said, "Drop your pants."

Grabbing my manhood with her fingernails up caused me to recoil, knocking down the screen. The embarrassment was hers sitting there holding my penis in her hand to be witnessed by the grinning, wide-eyed Navy wives. The Navy doctor said he would have liked to have given me a Purple Heart with gold clustered gonads. At last, someone with a sense of humor!

The final blow to my ego was returning to the ship and checking in with the Chief Medical Corpsman to report what had happened. He asked me to drop my pants and undershorts. Then, to his shock, he saw that the Navy doctor had attached a sling around my penis, as a joke, much the way one wears a sling with a broken arm. I was put on three days of light duty as my reward." (end of John's account) Mixed into that scenario were some lighter moments when a liberty boat full of inebriated sailors returned to the ship from the enlisted men's club on shore. The officers were no exception. On one occasion, the officers from an aircraft carrier purchased drinks for all officers from every ship for the entire evening in the officers club. But that was no big deal when drinks were only 10 cents each.

One evening, around 11:00, when the liberty launches were returning to the ship, a boatload of loud, inebriated sailors pulled up at the Goodrich 's quarterdeck. The sailors stormed aboard and the OOD had trouble controlling things, when, suddenly, one sailor fell overboard. There was great confusion and shouting to get the drunken sailor fished out before he got bitten by the prevalent barracudas.

The next day, when the Goodrich was in the middle of a submarine depth charge attack, a voice came up on the bridge talker's phone: " Your sonar shack has just been blown apart by a bomb!" It turned out that two UDT infiltrators had joined the launch full of sailors the night before. One diverted attention by falling overboard and the other guy simply waltzed aboard, unnoticed, and hid in the sonar shack that night. The captain was furious when he received a negative mark on the ship's security.

Capt. Keegan was well liked by the officers and crew. Both sympathetic and understanding, yet he expected things to be conducted in an orderly fashion, according to regulation. Coming from the submarine service, he knew that, but he also had things to learn and master about destroyer ship handling.

In his personal life, however, he had gone through a difficult divorce. The minute the ship docked in port, he turned over command to the executive officer and disappeared on shore, not to return until it was time for the ship to sail. We quickly understood he was drowning his sorrows in the local bars. During one weekend between our two weeks of training at Guantánamo Bay, our ship journeyed to Kingston, Jamaica. We were tied up in a nest of three destroyers, outboard ships. After a hard week, those of us not on watch Sunday morning relished sleeping in late. But that dream soon evaporated. About 9:00 a.m., the ship's loudspeakers blared out, "All officers report to the wardroom at 12:00 noon in dress blues." Imagine, the heavy woolen blue uniform in the hot tropics.

When we arrived in the wardroom, the executive officer informed us that the captain was bringing aboard four visitors at 12:15 p.m. Sure enough, at the appointed time, there came the captain, climbing up and down ladders to get across the two ships that were nested closer to the pier. Following behind him were four prostitutes, in very high heels, and attired in the most brightly colored, gaudy outfits you have ever seen. They were all heavily made up and wearing bright red lipstick. There we were with the captain, his four lady friends, and about six officers sitting together in the wardroom. We were unable to converse since the ladies spoke only Spanish. To make matters worse, we couldn't even offer a drink because all we had was coffee. The captain was pretty far gone, and these ladies had become his closest friends. I'm sure the sailors on all three ships got a real eyeful and laughed up a storm.

But Leo and I weren't much better. On a similar excursion from Guantanamo, the Goodrich anchored off St. Thomas, Virgin Islands, and we both had liberty at the same time. Our first goal was to rent a taxi and journey over the mountains and down the northside of St. Thomas to Magen Bay. It was remote, no people anywhere. We told the taxi driver he would collect the second half of his fee when he returned at 5:00 p.m. to get us. It was the most beautiful cove, about one kilometer across, with a pure-white sandy beach, light green clear water, which was ringed by a lush palm tree jungle. Regarding the acoustics, one could stand at one end of the beach and be heard perfectly at the other end. The water temperature was perfect and we soaked up too much sun all day.

At 5:00 p.m., the taxi came to fetch us, and we directed him to the Bluebeard Castle nightclub at the top of the mountain. Others from the ship said they would meet us there for dinner.

The stage entertainment didn't start until 9:00 p.m., when it was dark and things cooled down. You can imagine how many rum drinks Leo and I consumed. We were totally sloshed from the double whammy of sun all day and the rum. When the entertainment began, it seemed tepid and dull, so we mounted the stage and started singing Cornell drinking songs with loud bass voices. We felt the manager would reward us for adding some real good entertainment. But he was of a different mind and called the Shore Patrol. To our total dismay, Lt. Cdr. Wrocklage, Executive officer of the Goodrich and several SP Sailors from our ship, quickly escorted us out to the SP wagon.

The next thing I remember was being shoved into a captain's gig, or ship's motor whaleboat, and we headed out to sea to the anchorage.

Between the rum and the rolling boat, as the waves to seaward got bigger, Leo and I sang more songs as vigorously as possible to avoid throwing up. The boat approached the first destroyer at anchor, and I gratefully scrambled up the vertical Jacob's ladder and looked the OOD straight in

the face and said, "You're not on the fucking Goodrich!"
He replied, "That's right, and you can just climb right back
down the ladder!" I don't remember how we made it to
our ship without losing it all.

CHAPTER 5

Before I Reported On Board

As I recounted before, my close colleague, Leo Chamberlain, graduated in 1952 and reported aboard the *Goodrich* one year ahead of my arrival. Moreover, all the officers on board in 1952 who had achieved the rank of LT (jg), comprised the core of the seasoned officer complement. They were primarily responsible for passing on the experience that a year later shaped my destiny. Of course, this was with the exception of the three more senior officers, namely, the captain, the executive officer, and the operations officer.

As Leo recounts:

"I'm beginning to think I was the only June graduate (1952) to arrive on the *Goodrich* when it was in pristine condition. In fact, I recall the ship's first assignment after I came on board was to escort the S.S. *United States* cruise ship into New York harbor on its maiden visit."

I was very impressed until Black Jack Nuttall made me do something stupid. On my first midshipman cruise in 1949, there was a group of sailors huddled around a galvanized pail partially filled with water. They were shaking it and yelling, "Fish! fish!" If you bent over to see the fish you got whacked in the rear end with a paddle. Of course, I bent over. On an early day on the *Goodrich*, a pail appeared along with the same routine. I demurred, wanting to know what was intended. Black Jack was standing nearby and said, "Go look at the fish." I said I knew otherwise and didn't want to be whacked. He replied that it was for the men's morale, so go look at the fish. As a result, I got whacked and avoided contact with Nuttall as much as possible after that.

Soon after arriving on board, the XO, Black Jack Nuttall, sent me to the Gunnery Department Officer, Dick Husty. Upon discussing my limited qualifications and experience, he assigned me to the first division, located at the bow. The next morning, I attended my first quarter meeting. Standing before the sailors, I began, "Men!" Unfortunately, my voice cracked, and the word came out in two syllables. There was snickering and smug grins on the faces of the sailors. A voice from the rear roared, "Oh boy, we got another pansy OCS guy!" Although humiliated, I got through the meeting and huddled with the three CPOs in the division: a gunnery mate chief, a boatswain's mate chief, and a fire control mate chief.

I asked the chiefs who held their liberty cards. They replied that it was me, the division officer. I asked them if they would like to hold the cards themselves. They said they would like that. I responded, "I expect a sharp division and quiet quarters in the future. Here are your cards." Both my requests were granted.

Soon thereafter, Ezra Bixby, an English major from Princeton, came on board to relieve Dick Young as Electronics Repair Officer. Since I was an EE graduate, I preferred that billet over that of czar of the deck apes. I asked Ezra if he would like to add to his already prodigious vocabulary. I told him I heard words at the first division that were new to me, and he might have had the same experience. He wasn't eager to go the electronics route so we switched billets with the new XO LT CDR Hemmingsen approving. I spent three years as ERO and had the pleasure of working with some of the brightest sailors on board, the electronics technicians.

The *Goodrich* departed its home base in Newport, Rhode

Island, on January 1953, to spend five months assigned to the Sixth Fleet, which was stationed in the Mediterranean. Typically, each ship would spend a week underway with various task units of the Sixth Fleet conducting training maneuvers and patrols, and then spend the alternate week tied up in different ports in the Mediterranean: Portugal, Gibraltar, Spain, France, Italy, and Greece.

On March 20, 1953 the Sixth Fleet was engaged in Operation Rendezvous. During this operation, a task unit of ships were conducting darken ship, a night time carrier operation. On that occasion, Leo was OOD (Officer of the Deck) on the midwatch (00:00 - 04:00). The *Goodrich* was directed to take a plane guard position on the carrier U.S.S. Midway. The CIC (Combat Information Center), where a third officer on watch manned the radar room below) and I came up with two solutions for our reorientation: one around the screen of destroyers surrounding the "heavies," and a more direct route through the formation, which was at darken ship. I awakened Captain Hayler to ask him which approach he preferred. He said, "We're a destroyer so we'll take the direct approach." As OOD, I had the con, and ordered a course change to start us on our way. A few minutes passed and the captain asked if my intention was to pass the heavy cruiser Newport News ahead or astern. I didn't know how he could see her with darken ship, but I told him "astern." He replied, "Then you'd better come left." I called in the pilot house, "Left full rudder." We were out on the open bridge and the Newport News loomed up in front of us. We were coming left rapidly. As we passed their stern, the stern light came on, which lit up our bridge sufficiently to see the expression of horror on our sailors' faces. I remembered to tell the helmsman, "Shift your rudder" in order to take a course parallel to the formation behind the U.S.S. Midway. I didn't sleep that night.

The next day the Admiral sent Captain Hayler a message letting him know we had had a close call. The captain, calm as a cucumber, told the Admiral he was letting his OOD take her through and was a little late turning left.

LT (jg) Bruce Tharp also talked about the cool, calm demeanor of Captain Hayler "A similar situation occurred on the '53 Med cruise when Hayler was captain. On that occasion, Hayler came out unnoticed from the sea cabin. I was not aware of his presence until I heard him ask in a very soft, calm voice what was going on. I turned around to see him standing quietly behind me, looking over my shoulder. I told him about the maneuver in progress, and went on with it. Once or twice he asked softly and calmly, "Do you think you should come right a little?"

Hayler was an uncanny ship handler. At the time, I was OOD, but Hayler had the con. We were directed to assume the lifeguard station 1000 yards astern when we finished. The captain said he would keep the con, then pulled away with a 180 degree turn using hard right rudder. Then, the same thing: another right hard rudder turn. As the ship steadied in a position dead astern of the carrier, he turned to me with a slight smile and said, "You have the con, Mr. Tharp." When I took a range, the carrier was exactly 1000 yards at 000 degrees relative bearing to the stern of the carrier. At that point, it was easy to bring the ship a bit to the right, so that the ship was positioned 15 defrees off the stern, or giving a relative bearing of 345 degrees to the stern of the carrier. The purpose of this position is that sometimes planes attempting to land on the carrier, come in too low, and ditch into the sea. For that reason, the plane guard destroyer will not run over the pilot and his plane, and can put engines full astern to stop and pick him up.

Something similar occurred when we were coming in to anchor in Menton, my favorite port. As Hayler had the con and was directing the ship to the anchorage, we lost steering control and shifted to after steering. But they could not take control back there, for reasons I don't recall. No worries. Hayler maneuvered us directly to the spot using the engines. That may or may not be a big deal, but it sure impressed me at the time and was one of the many incidents that helped put the man up on my personal pantheon of ship handlers.

Anyone would have suffered by comparison, and Captain Keegan, Hayler's replacement, certainly did, especially with regard to keeping his cool. It happened again later under Captain Neff, with quite different consequences (recounted later).

But then, just to provide another perspective, Hayler bought a sailboat somewhere (I don't remember where) and had it lashed to the superstructure. He could hardly wait to take it for a sail at the next port and signed on one of the officers as crew to help with that. The boat had a really tall mast and looked a little ungainly as they sailed away. It was not long before a wind gust came along and blew the sail and mast into the water. Efforts to right her were unsuccessful. When Captain Hayler got back on board, he was not a happy sailor. He was pretty embarrassed, and, as I recall, the incident was never discussed in the wardroom in his presence.

There was little opportunity for recreation or sports. So the *Goodrich* had a softball team in 1953 consisting of between nine and eleven sailors and one officer, me. We had uniforms and were anxious to face the world. The first game during our Med Cruise was in Gibraltar. I didn't record in my journal who we played or who won. Probably the other team won or I would have recorded the score. The next game was in Palermo, where we lost 12 to 5 to the U.S.S. Larson. Then, in Ajaccio, we beat the U.S.S. Tarawa twice, three to two and nine to three. Afterwards, we reached Augusta Bay. We were transported to a small landing next to the ball field in the captain's gig since that was our only mode of transportation when we were anchored. We played the U.S.S. Newport News and lost. At the end of the game, it was getting a little dark and chilly. Remember, this was February 22. Since the gig had not returned, we asked the coxswain of the cruiser's motor launch if he would please drop us off at the *Goodrich* on his way to the Newport News. He said that his orders were to pick up the team and return to the ship, so he refused our request. We were stuck. No gig appeared. We were surrounded by teenage Sicilian boys who wanted to sell us wine for one dollar a bottle.

Reluctantly, we agreed because we were getting colder. We drank a few bottles. We decided to find the main landing to get a ride back to the ship since there still was no gig. We staggered through what appeared to be a war-torn area of bombed-out buildings until we finally found a road. We located the landing and were told by the senior shore patrol officer to get on one of the motor launches, which was about to leave. Before we embarked, I counted heads and found that Seaman Santangelo was absent. As a result, I explained to the shore patrol officer, who was a LT CDR, that we first should find Santangelo. He said, "Get on the boat!" I said, "Sir, you don't understand, one of our men is missing." He retorted, "I told you to get on the Goddamned boat!" My unfortunate reply was, "Stick the boat up your ass!" He said, "You're on report. Go sit in that tent." The motor launch left with the men, and I was sitting in a tent, giving my name. Since we were not in uniform, no one knew I was an officer. They just wanted my name. They put me on a motor launch filled with marine SPs and returned me to the *Goodrich* with one half of a "report chit," the other half being forwarded to Sixth Fleet Headquarters in Naples. When we arrived at the *Goodrich* gangplank, Ezra Bixby was sitting on the top step holding his stomach in a frenzied laughing fit. A marine escorted me to the deck and gave Ezra the chit. I went to bed.

The next morning at breakfast in the wardroom, I was badly hung over. My shipmates were commiserating with me about my short-lived naval career and wondered what punishment would be meted out. I was concerned about a possible Bad Conduct Discharge. Finally, they admitted that Bob Chidsey had gone back to the landing and talked the LT CDR out of the "other half" of the chit. So I was saved to sin again.

LT (jg) Bruce Tharp, who was OOD that day, completes the story of Leo's arrest: "Unlike some destroyers at the time, the *Goodrich* had only one motor whaleboat, appropriately referred to as "The Captain's Gig." I had been OOD that afternoon when the gig was dispatched to take the softball team to its game. Later on my watch, Captain Hayler called for the gig to take him to some kind of party at an officer's club on the beach. The order to the coxswain was to take the Captain ashore and return. Instead, as was his prerogative, Hayler preempted the previous order and told the coxswain to wait for him. They waited quite a while. As a result, there was no gig on hand when the time came to pick up the team. All I could do was nervously wait for it to return and, as night fell, wonder what the softball team was doing."

I was among the group that assembled on the quarterdeck when the word went around that Leo was in sight. I could see him approaching in a big motor launch in which he and his Marine escort were the only passengers. I can tell you that as they drew near Leo could be heard directing his "up your ass" comments to anyone in earshot. Bixby tried to placate the Marine by explaining the circumstances and thereby talking him out of forwarding a report, to no avail. Apparently, Chidsey had to finish the job the next day. I had forgotten about that.

The episodes of the baseball team and our behavior were not always confined to Naval personnel or the shore patrol. As Leo further recounts:

"The ship's softball team continued to play at ports where there was less interest in other shore activities. So we played in Lisbon during the midshipmen cruise. Since we were tied up to a pier, we were able to take a local taxi to the ball field. This was no small feat as the taxi driver spoke little if any English.

After wild gesticulations, swinging of bats and pounding of gloves, the driver signaled his understanding and off we went. When we arrived at the field there were more wild gesticulations, pointing at watches, running around a circle twice (signifying two hours), waving goodbye and finally a nod that he understood he was to leave and return in two hours.

"We played our game, which was uneventful, packed up our gear and looked for the taxi. He was right where we had left him with the meter running. Then he demanded an exorbitant fee to return to the ship. We went looking for another taxi. Before we found one, a Portuguese police paddy wagon appeared with cops holding machine guns. He had called the cops. They signaled us to enter the paddy wagon (still no English). We did so and were driven to the local police station. It was not the same one to which I was assigned the night before so there was no translator. We were put in a jail cell; 11 miscreants in uniform and all cold sober and feeling very righteous although apprehensive given the machine guns and no English anywhere.

"After a couple of hours of cooling our heels, a nice young man from the United States Consulate showed up and negotiated our release after we paid the taxi driver his ill-gotten gains. It seems a lady heard the altercation at the field, understood both Portuguese and English, and saw us drive off in the paddy wagon. So she called the Consulate to report the "misunderstanding." She showed up at the jail and explained she had lived in New Bedford at one time. We asked the man from the Consulate if she could be awarded the Medal of Freedom. He said, 'No.'

"When we returned to the ship, the XO told us we could have caused an international incident. We said, 'The guy shouldn't have tried to cheat us!' "

As Leo remembers, there were also Sixth Fleet Social events:

"During the 1953 Med Cruise, LT (jg) Bob Michaels and I decided to celebrate my 23rd birthday with a few drinks when we were at Piraeus, Greece. The XO said there was a reception planned for the Sixth Fleet by the Greek government and that drinks would be free. So we donned our dress blues and took a taxi to the reception. There were signs in English directing us down a long hallway. On both sides of the hallway Greek soldiers dressed in their short white skirts were standing at ease. As we drew parallel to them they snapped to attention, clicked their heels and held their rifles in front of them 'at arms.' As we passed, they returned to at ease. We were both impressed and slightly intimidated.

"When we reached the reception area, we were shocked to see there was no naval rank below a LT CDR standing around the hors d'oeuvres. There were several four stripers and an Admiral. We slinked to the side and tried to stay out of sight. We began to eat the shrimp and drink the punch. After a while, we became a little inebriated. Just as the hum of conversation seemed to stop as is sometimes the case in a crowded room, I said to Bob in a fairly loud voice, 'You know, Bob, you're not a bad guy for an Annapolis snot!' A CDR came to our side and told us it was time to return to our ship.

"The next day, the XO made us go to the bridge and stand lookout duty even though we were in a nest of destroyers at a pier. We didn't see anything to report, but our heads hurt too much to focus properly."

During his first Med cruise, Leo was still totally obsessed with his new bride. Consequently, he rejected the pleas of his fellow officers to go ashore and taste the fruits of life on the French Riviera. But before departing the Med, he was finally convinced to go ashore and buy his wife, Leah, some French lingerie.

He recalls:

"I found a shop that sold lingerie, looked in the window and walked right in. The sales lady did not speak English, and I had but two years of High School French, so the confrontation was on." I grabbed my chest to show I wanted to buy a brassiere. The shop lady asked me what size? I replied, 'Trente-deux.' She looked at me strangely and asked if the bra was for my daughter. I said that it was for my wife. She said, 'Impossible,' and I got a little testy and said not all Americans have big tits. She then showed me a brassiere that was more of the size she envisioned. It was an 84! You see, French bra sizes are measured in centimeters. My wife said, upon receipt, that she never expected to be a size 84!"

Leo was always "pushing the envelope" of practical jokes. He tells about plane guarding:

"We were on plane guard duty during the 1953 Med Cruise which meant we were 1000 yards astern of an aircraft carrier that was launching and landing F4Us. It was important to stay on station because the pilots, when turning onto the glide path to land on the carriers, used us as a guide on their way to the carrier deck.

"There was little wind that day so the carrier had to crank it up in excess of 30 knots, which was faster than the *Goodrich* could go. The engine order telegraph mechanism on the bridge had Flank as the maximum speed setting so I decided to improvise to catch up to the carrier, which was leaving us (and the pilots) in the dust.

"The sailor standing watch on the engine telegraph was a teenage, inexperienced seaman. He was confused when I called out an order, 'All ahead Bendix, turns for 35 knots.' The manufacturer of the telegraph was Bendix Corporation, and their name on the telegraph just beyond the Flank setting. There was no way to move the telegraph indicator past Flank, but the young sailor on the engine order didn't know this, so he strained to try to move the indicator past Flank to Bendix.

"As he was pushing on the telegraph handle, the captain came on the bridge. He noticed the sailor trying to move the telegraph lever and said, 'Son, what are you trying to do?' The sailor replied, 'I'm trying to get the handle into Bendix so we can get up to 35 knots.' The captain then asked, 'Does Mr. Chamberlain have the con?' After an affirmative answer, the captain joined me on the open bridge and said, 'Leo, don't play jokes on the bridge!' "

Even the captain was not immune. Leo loved to tell about the captain's coffee:

"The captain often ordered a cup of coffee from the wardroom when he was on the bridge. Unfortunately, the wardroom was three decks below the bridge and connected by a very steep set of ladders. As a consequence, the steward had difficulty climbing the ladders without the coffee spilling onto the saucer if filled too full, or would be half a cup to avoid overflowing. The captain never failed to berate the steward who was bringing the coffee because of spilled coffee, or getting just half a cup.

"One day I noticed the cups presented to the captain were full and not spilled. I thought the steward was bringing a pitcher along with the cup and pouring out the proper amount at the top of the ladder. So Iasked one of the sailors if the steward had a pitcher with him when he appeared at the bridge. 'Oh no, he has a better method.' It seems he pours in the proper amount at the bottom of the ladders, takes a mouthful without swallowing, runs up the ladder, and spits the contents of his mouth back into the cup, resulting in a full cup, and thereby keeping the captain in good spirits!"

LT (jg) Bruce Tharp was another one of my senior mentors and served earlier and concurrently with Leo. He recalls the following:" My emotions on first reporting on board the *Goodrich* and the early days thereafter were very close to what you, Max, described as yours.

"It was June of 1951. I had taken the overnight train from Philadelphia to Boston, with all my Navy-related worldly goods packed into one enormous suitcase. It was known as the Samsonite Seven-Suiter, which was extremely heavy. This was long before anyone had thought of putting wheels on luggage, of course. The cab from South Station dropped me off at the main gate of the Navy Yard, at which I learned the location of the dock to which the

Goodrich was tied up. It was quite a hike. It was a very warm day, and the seven-suiter got heavier as I made my way toward active duty. I arrived at the ship around 0900 in my brand new dress khakis, now pretty soggy with perspiration. My reaction was just like yours. It was a mess! Red lead paint on much of the surfaces, wires dangling everywhere, various tools scattered about, etc. This was not what I had imagined as my entry into Navy duty.

"As I prepared to go aboard, I reviewed all I had been taught about doing so -- approach the OOD, give him a snappy salute, and tell him you are reporting aboard for duty. The trouble was, I could not see anyone resembling an officer, let alone one in charge. The closest I could come was a guy in dungarees with a belt and 45 pistol around his waist, and a second class gunner's mate insignia on his sleeve. I focused on this slight indication of authority and told him who I was. He sent a seaman with a pistol-less belt (whom I later realized had been the messenger on watch) to fetch someone and soon a guy in wrinkled work khakis with lieutenant's bars on his collar came down the main deck and introduced himself as Lou Baldwin. He was the Chief Engineer -- the start of a lineage that went through Jack Smith, Craig Smith, Al Shapiro and, eventually, Max Bosshardt.

"He took me to the wardroom and sat with me making small talk until the gunnery officer, Andy Shreve, arrived and told me I had been assigned to the Gunnery Department and took me to my stateroom. I had anticipated something a cut above the cubicle with three bunks that was just forward of the wardroom and one deck down and was incredibly hot. I got out my wash khakis, unpacked the rest of my stuff, and, with great difficulty, found a place for my large piece of luggage with the help of my roommate, Jim Hossfeld, a recent Academy graduate also newly arrived and assigned to Gunnery. I then made my way topside and started my active duty. I was pretty disillusioned by the semi-chaos I saw about me, a far cry from the formality and organization that my NROTC training had prepared me for.

"I had not read The Caine Mutiny before coming aboard, but did so soon thereafter and it really depressed me. As I went through the saga of Willie Keith, I saw many things that struck home regarding what was going on about me, and I secretly despaired about the days ahead. That was reinforced by the person of the exec, J. J. Nuttall, a.k.a. Black Jack, who closely resembled the Caine's Captain Queeg. But, as I made friends and got into the far-cry-from-sea-duty shipyard routine, those feelings disappeared. It was extremely helpful in that to become fully involved with my first assigned duty. That involved being put in charge of the Coke machine on the main deck, with the help of a seaman who was assigned to do the basic stuff, mostly making sure it was kept full. But, that's another story."

It seems that there are countless steps along the career path for green young ensigns to get seasoned. For example, Bruce also recalls another incident: "During the 1952 Med cruise, while we were anchored in the Bay of Naples, I was called upon to deliver some kind of documents to the Sixth Fleet flag office. I don't recall the nature of the stuff, nor the flag vessel (other than the obvious fact it was some cruiser or another -- come to think of it, it may have been the Salem). Anyway, as the *Goodrich* MWB approached the ship, the coxswain headed for the forward gangway to deliver me. Just as I stepped onto the lower platform of the gangway, I was startled to hear a band on the deck above break out in martial music, followed by the shrill whistle of a bosun's pipe. My wonderment about what was going on increased when I looked up to see a gaggle of side boys snap salutes. But at the same time I also saw the OOD in dress blues with a long telescope under his arm standing at the top of the gangway vigorously gesticulating in a way that made it clear I should get my butt back in the boat and shove off. I did just that as the music precipitously stopped in mid-measure. My coxswain then circled around to the after gangway and I went aboard. I was told by the JOOD back there that my boat had been mistaken for one which was bringing the Mayor of Naples or some such dignitary for a visit and folks forward were pretty ticked off about the embarrassment associated with the false alarm I had created. The lesson for me involved a reinforcement of the concept that there is a difference between the forward and after gangways on a ship of that size. But I felt pretty innocent of any wrongdoing, figuring that the OOD should have been able to tell the difference between a MWB with 831 on the bow and the one he was expecting, particularly given the availability of that fancy telescope under his arm."

Bruce commits a serious "no no": "Missing the sailing of a ship was a serious matter. So when it happened to me, albeit for a relatively short trip within the confines of Narragansett Bay, I was filled with apprehension about the fate that awaited me once I made it back to the *Goodrich*. But I was saved from whatever fate would have been mine by the intervention of Ezra Bixby. Here's the story":

"It happened one morning in Newport. In those days there were no docks there at which ships could be berthed. Instead, destroyers moored to buoys located throughout the near part of Narragansett Bay in "nests.""

These involved several ships (usually four) that were tied up to each other and individually connected to a large buoy with a section of anchor chain. With this arrangement the only way to get to the beach was via the ship's motor whaleboat. Conventional destroyers had two such boats. But because of the upper deck configuration associated with the *Goodrich* 's configuration as a radar picket destroyer, we had room for only one, known as the Captain's Gig. So, our ability to go back and forth to the beach was somewhat limited under the best of conditions. When foul weather restricted boating, as it regularly did, we were unable to leave the ship and there were a lot of unhappy sailors on board come liberty time.

"On this day, in the summer of 1952, the *Goodrich* was scheduled to move from its buoy location to go alongside a destroyer tender that was moored to a pier up the bay so that we could use the services of the tender for routine maintenance. That was an event we were all looking forward to because it meant we would spend two weeks alongside a pier, where we would be able to get home easily when we did not have the duty. Many of us in the wardroom, including me, had recently been married and getting home to our wives at night was important. "I woke at home that foggy morning with the horrible realization that I had overslept and was in danger of missing the last scheduled boat to the *Goodrich*. I threw on my uniform and drove recklessly through the fog with my wife to the Fleet Landing. Once there, I could see the *Goodrich* gig disappearing into the mist on the last scheduled trip to the *Goodrich* before it got underway for the tender. At the landing making preparations to cast off was a gig from a destroyer in the nest next to ours. In desperation I tried to convince the coxswain to divert and drop me off at the *Goodrich*. Of course, I realized that request was in vain -- coxswains are obligated not to deviate from the orders given by the officer of the deck (OOD) when initially dispatched, but I was in a "nothing ventured, nothing gained" situation. Naturally, he turned me down. But I was able to convince him to allow me to go along on his return to his ship, where I could ask the OOD if I could get a lift over to the *Goodrich* in its nearby nest. Once there, I was told that was impossible because his captain was waiting for the gig at the landing. All they could do was take me back ashore. So it was back to the fleet landing, where my wife was waiting to see how the situation played out. "With a heavy heart I told her we would have to drive up the bay so I could board the *Goodrich* after it had tied up alongside the tender. The heavy heart came from the intuition that 'missing ship,' even for a short trip up the bay, was a serious offense. I expected that once I was on board, the consequences were going to be at least restriction to the ship for the two-week period alongside the tender, thus missing out on the luxury of getting home easily on the two evenings out of three I did not have the duty.

"As we drove up the road alongside Narragansett Bay, the fog was lifting. I could see the *Goodrich* steaming north to the tender as I inwardly groaned at the circumstances responsible and the fate that awaited me. We drove down to the dock and waited. My angst grew as the other three ships scheduled for maintenance tied up alongside the tender. (The *Goodrich 's* captain was the junior CO of the four ships involved, which made her the farthest from the dock.) As the *Goodrich* made her way to take her place, I told my bride this was no doubt goodbye for at least two weeks and set off to go aboard. I made my way onto the tender, then across the three ships already in place. "As soon as the gangway between ships was put down, I walked aboard the *Goodrich* and began slowly making my way to the wardroom to face the consequences of my actions. When I came out of the amidships passageway and started forward on the port side of the main deck, I saw the Executive Officer approaching and began steeling myself for his words. Gritting my teeth, I gave him a smart salute and a "Good morning, sir." I was dumbfounded as, in a normal tone of voice, he said, 'Good morning, Mr. Tharp. How are you this morning?' and continued on his way aft as if all were right with the world. "And so it was! When I went into the wardroom, Bixby was there. 'Where the hell were you?' he asked. And then I learned why the exec had been his usual cordial self. Here's what happened. As a CIC (Combat Information Center) officer, my normal duty station for Special Sea Detail, the condition that was in place while the ship was underway in inland waters, was in CIC, the site of the ship's major radar capability. There, I was responsible for overseeing radar support to navigation and relaying appropriate information to the bridge. When Bixby, whom I believe was assistant CIC officer at the time, realized I was not on board he stood in for me in CIC and generated the information relayed to the bridge. Since that information was sent up via a telephone talker, no one on the bridge realized I was not at my post and I was never missed!"

So, Bixby saved me from at least a miserable couple of weeks confined to the ship away from my bride or, possibly, worse. He probably put his own hide in jeopardy as well. He was a good friend.

CHAPTER 6

Qualifying As O.O.D.

The rigorous training schedule at Guantanamo in the fall of 1953 was just the beginning! Upon returning to our home port in Newport, Rhode Island, we spent the next six months steaming out every other week to take part in joint exercises as part of multi-ship task units, or larger groups.

On one of our first sorties in the Atlantic, I was assigned to stand JOOD watch, or junior officer of the deck, under my notorious mentor, LTJ(jg) Ezra Bixby. By that time, I had stood JOOD watches a good dozen times and had some inkling of what I was expected to do. While the OOD has full responsibility to give orders for maneuvering the ship, the JOOD had to assist him by interpreting any flag signals from the command ship, or plot a course and direction to a new station in the formation, check ranges to the guide ship on the radar.

Bixby, a large, rollicking redhead from Boston, had wonderful self-confidence. During one particular watch section our ship was on the right hand outboard station in a bent line anti-submarine screen, ahead of several heavy ships composed of the flagship, a heavy cruiser, and an oil tanker. Suddenly, without warning, Bixby ordered me to "take the con," and assume responsibility as the OOD. It was my first time, and a shiver ran down my spine. In my best commanding voice, I announced to the helmsman, engine order telegraph man, and other sailors on the bridge that "I have the con," and they knew I would be issuing orders from that point on.

Shortly thereafter, the signalman called down from the signal bridge, "The flagship has raised the pennants," turn nine", sir.' Maneuvering orders from the flagship were typically sent by signal flags so there could be no advanced notice to enemy ships about our maneuvers. When the flags were hauled down on the flagship, the signalman would shout "execute," indicating that the maneuver was to begin. In this particular case there had not been a prior order to reorient the bent line submarine screen of some six destroyers in the direction of the new course. The signal simply meant that upon execution all ships were to make a 90° turn to the right.

In a few minutes I heard the signalman call down "execute," and to haul down our own pennants. With the best commanding voice I could muster, I ordered "right standard rudder" to the helmsman. With 20° rudder, the Goodrich began a beautiful curve to the right, coming to a new course 90° from the old course. But then I was horror struck. We had departed from the task unit, which seemed to be steaming forward on the old course. Almost immediately, a light signal in Morse Code came from the flagship. "Wireworm (that was our call sign), get back on station." About that time Captain Keegan came racing around the pilothouse shouting at me "Max, where the hell are you going?" I don't even remember what Bixby was doing, but I learned a lesson under terribly humiliating circumstances. When steaming with heavy ships, a destroyer should only use about 5° rudder and constantly check the range to the flagship because the heavy ships take much longer to make a turn with their standard rudder. The captain relieved me of the watch on the spot, sent me below, and ordered me to report to the executive officer for additional instruction. It was a tough lesson. Bruce mentioned Captain Keegan's hypertension at ship handling. I think he was right!

We spent part of 1954 going out in the Atlantic on "Operation Springboard," involving large numbers of ships. During this time, I became qualified as OOD. I was once summarily relieved of the con as OOD and sent below. For two hours in the Atlantic, two large task groups were approaching each other at right angles, to eventually merge. They arrived early, so our speed was cut to less than 5 knots. The *Goodrich* was the outboard ship of a bent line screen, and we slowly approached the corresponding ship of the other group. For an hour we slowly closed range before the formation change execution was given. We were still a good half mile away when suddenly

Captain Keegan woke up, came out of the sea cabin, half asleep, and spotted the other ship and screamed, "We're on a collision course. I have the con!" Oh well. The exec had to give me a special pseudo lecture on ship exercises!

The other incident was hairier. The *Goodrich* and another tin can were exercising as a two-ship ("brother /sister") hunter-killer group with a sub in about March 1954. I was the OOD. We had just passed over the sub, fired center (dropping our depth charges off the stern), and Captain Keegan, as group leader, on the port side of the bridge, announced over the radio to the other destroyer: "I have fired center, I am sister, you are bother, I am coming left." The other ship was off our starboard bow moving left. At that moment I had just given the helm the order: "Hard right rudder!" I shouted over to Captain Keegan that I was coming right, not left. He bypassed me and told the helmsman, "SHIFT THE RUDDER!" By this time we were rapidly approaching the port side of sister, which was taking evasive action and turning right. I forget, but I think we must have shifted rudder once or twice more. We passed sister by only 100 feet.

The entire hunter killer tactic is based on the fact that when a destroyer passes over a submarine, its sonar becomes ineffective. As it approaches the target, it has to estimate the right moment to drop depth charges. In order not to lose contact with the submarine, the sister ship of the hunter killer group circles around the attack point on a circle with a diameter of 1000 yards, where it is able to maintain sonar contact with the submarine. Then, as soon as the brother ship has fired center, the group leader designates that ship as sister, and the other ship as brother, which then commences another depth charge attack over the submarine There are rules to follow for the ship that has just fired center. This is done in order to determine which way to turn to keep out of the way of the sister ship, which then is turning in toward the sub's position to make the next depth charge run. Obviously, Captain Keegan made an error in telling the other ship he was coming left, when that sister ship was on our starboard bow also moving left, and he should have consulted me, the OOD, to find out what orders I had given the helm.

Many years later, in 2012, two photographs appeared in the issue of the Tin Can Sailor newsletter showing this incident of a near collision from the viewpoint of the sister ship. It happened that a sailor, Ed Freketic, was standing on the stern of the USS Hunt, DD 674, had a camera and recorded the incident. I later submitted a letter to the editor of the Tin Can Sailor explaining the true details of what happened.

Photo taken from the US S Hunt, as Goodrich almost collides with the Hunt.

Another part of our training consisted of executing a man overboard drill. I was OOD on one occasion when the word was passed up to the bridge, "man overboard, port side." For the exercise, the exec had thrown over a life ring to simulate a man in the water. I then commenced the standard procedure and ordered 15 knot speed and right full rudder. It is quicker to retrieve the man out of the water by making a full circle at 15 knots and then stopping than it is to stop the ship first and then trying to back down to reach the spot where the man was. The captain was on the bridge observing the procedure. In my own mind, I knew that when we got around the full circle, I would have to use my binoculars to search for the man because I already needed glasses with my 20/40 vision. So I told the helmsman to call out his heading every 10 degrees. When he reached 340°, or 20° shy of our original course, I stopped all engines. At 350° around, I ordered back full on both engines. At 360° I ordered the engines stopped. It was a bit wavy at sea that day and easy for the object to be obscured periodically with waves. I was searching frantically with my binoculars to find the object in the water, but of course my field of vision was limited through the binoculars. At that point the captain tapped me on the shoulder, and said, "Max, he's over there," pointing quite a bit to the left of where I was looking. Another learning incident that one never forgets.

CHAPTER 7

Chief Engineer School

I think one must marvel at the degree of training that takes place, which can accommodate a change of every ship's personnel by 50 percent, approximately every two years! This not only demands rapid qualification in one's assigned function, but a rapid progression in the degree of responsibility one must assume. This upward mobility far exceeds that which one would experience starting out in a civilian job, in a corporation.

In my own case, I had academic education as an electrical engineer. However, my exposure to the specific details of a US Navy ship's main propulsion plant was really quite limited. During one summer cruise, I rotated through operating positions in the machinery room and boiler room of a heavy cruiser. During school, I had one course in Naval Science each semester, but only one year of that course was dedicated to ships engineering plants. Then, reporting on board the *Goodrich,* I was assigned as Electrical Officer during the shipyard overall, and three months later upon departure to Guantánamo, and due to the departure of the Chief Engineer, I was already promoted to Main Propulsion Assistant, or the number two job in the engineering department.

Thus, by spring of 1954, in my second year on board, I had already qualified as Officer of the Deck, and was destined to become one of four department heads, namely, Chief Engineer. As final preparation for this promotion, I was sent to a 12 week training course on another destroyer stationed in Newport, Rhode Island, which acted as the engineering school ship. The training course was rigorous, thorough, and very intensive. During the first three weeks, we spent the entire morning each day preparing the main engineering plant to get underway, and every afternoon securing the main engineering plant. This was done by rotating through every operating position in the machinery and boiler spaces. Next came a week of maintenance, during which we disassembled major pumps, climbed inside the boilers and repaired the brickwork, and performed various other repair tasks. Another week was spent climbing all over the four engineering spaces and making a drawing of every valve controlling every steam and water line. The complexity came because each main engine, and all four boilers, could be connected in any combination

Another few weeks were spent going to sea at 0800 h. after the ship's crew had prepared to get underway. We steamed at sea all day long, again rotating through all the operating positions. And finally, the last week was spent operating the ship at sea and reacting to surprise emergency situations such as loss of burners in the boilers, rigging emergency electrical power, etc.

When I returned to the *Goodrich,* I was well-equipped to discuss any engineering propulsion system question with the 90 men who reported to me. They included Chief Petty Officer's, machinist mate's, boiler tenders, electricians mates, and telephone specialists. Of course, I did not have the depth of experience to actually work on the machinery as my men could, but on the other hand we formed a great team to make intelligent engineering decisions about the plant. I might add, that very few officers who reach the position of executive officer or commanding office of a ship, have had the same exposure to the engineering plant. Typically, they come up through the operations department or the gunnery department. Therefore, I felt in a very strong position vis a vis the captain when discussing a matter concerning the main propulsion plant.

Several incidents which occurred illustrate the point. I will relate these as they happened later in 1954 and 1956.

CHAPTER 8

European Midshipman Cruise

In the summer of 1954 the *USS Goodrich DDR-83 I* was assigned to a six ship task unit to take the Naval Academy Midshipmen on their summer cruise to Europe.

Leo recalls:

"During our first port of call, I found myself the senior shore patrol officer for a red light district of Lisbon. I was stationed in a Portuguese police station and had a translator cop assigned to me.

It occurred to me that I had never been in a whore house, nor would I probably ever have occasion to use one (being young and newly married). I decided to raid one to see what it was like "inside". I asked the cop if he knew where the largest house was in the district. He assured me he did, so I said, " we'll get the sailors out of there at 9 PM". He appeared flabbergasted and asked, "why? They'll all return later". I said, "be that as it may. The place is impure and I don't want the sailors to catch anything". The cop told me the girls were inspected daily for disease, but I retorted, " there's two kinds of impurity, physical and moral. Remember these boys have sisters and mothers!" The cop sighed and clucked his teeth.

At 9PM armed with a billy club and a whistle and backed by a half dozen incredulous SP sailors, I rapped my club on the front door. When it opened I blew my whistle and cried out, "this is a raid. Everyone out!" A number of sailors drinking beer out of bottles were sitting around a long table lighted up with ceiling spot lights. Two nude girls were about to get on the table when they were interrupted by yours truly. It was then I realized a better plan would have been to have someone inside. I ran down a hallway blowing my whisltle when I spotted a sailor wearing nothing but a T-shirt in front of me. I took pursuit and followed him into a courtyard with a metal circular staircase leading to another floor. At the top it occurred to me this pursuit wasn't wise so I hesitated banging the door at the top. Just then the door opened and my flashlight lighted up a nude girl who started to jabber at me in Potuguese so I backed off and returned to the main room to collect my entourage. The sailors had been saved. Their sisters and mothers would be pleased. The cop would recover in time. And I had visited my first and last whore house."

My memory of Captain Keegan was pleasant; always sober and on the job at sea. but ashore he was drowning his sorrows (divorce??) and drunk the whole time ashore, as Leo can attest:

"The first 2 hours of my shore patrol duty in Antwerpen during the 1954 Midshipmen Cruise of the *Goodrich* were uneventful Then as I passed a small bar on a side street I heard a familiar voice, " Hi Leo, come have a drink with me." It was Captain Keegan, sitting at a small table by himself three sheets to the wind. "But captain, I'm on shore patrol duty," said I. "Not to worry, just take off the SP band!" I really liked the captain, and didn't want to rebuff him, so I slipped off the SP band, sat down, and ordered a drink. Then I called over the two enlisted men on shore patrol with me and instructed them to go to the street corners to intercept any other SP's who may appear. They did so, chuckling merrily to themselves.

We had our drink, so I excused myself, snuck into the men's room, put the SP band back on and was relieved I had not soiled my underpants!" End of Leo's recollectons)

We had just departed Antwerpen, Belgium, and were two or three days at sea, totally occupied, not only with the usual watches and departmental work, but also dreaming up useful exercises for the Midshipmen. The flagship, a heavy cruiser, suddenly came alive and flashed out a Morse code message to all ships. Shortly thereafter, over the ship's loudspeakers, came the call : "all officers and chief petty officers report to the wardroom immediately."

I thought "oh no, one more crisis to crowd our time." The captain told us that the admiral had become aware that two first class midshipmen had taken delivery of several gross containers of hundreds of gift wrapped packages in Antwerpen. He believed that these were distributed to all ships in the task unit, with a sailor on each ship organizing the sale of such gifts. Each gift wrapped package was reported to contain seven pairs of nylon panties, colored Navy blue and gold, and each had a day of the week written on them.

A rather nice gift for a sailor to give his girlfriend, and a brilliant business scheme! Unfortunately, it is a Class A offense, threatening dismissal from the Naval Academy, for a midshipman to be conducting a private business!! So obviously, the admiral was on a witch hunt to find the reps and panties! He ordered a surprise inspection of all hands not on watch, to stand by their lockers, opened, at 15:00 hours. Department heads were to inspect every locker, accompanied by a Master at Arms CPO. I groaned. I had 90 men in my Engineering Department! What a waste of an hour or two looking at all those lockers.

As I started through the compartment, and had looked at roughly half of the lockers, I saw one off to the side, unattended, and still locked. AHA! Now I have found the culprit, and could end this nonsense. In a loud authoritative voice I asked "Who belongs to this locker??"

No answer. I then said "O.K. guys, we will remain standing here until the key appears". It was only a few moments when a sailor came forward, and said "Here is the key, Sir". Well, open it up I boomed. He did so, and to my shock and surprise, I saw a locker filled to the brim with cans of Tuna Fish!!!!

I stood in disbelief silence. Technically, I should report the man for stealing government property. But then I would be faced with filling out report forms and going to captain's mast with the sailor to have a hearing, and get his punishment. More hours would be wasted! Besides, I knew that when we take on stores from the supply ship, at sea, all hands are required to pass boxes of food below for storage, and each time a few boxes go astray, and disappear into the machinery spaces. After all, a man gets damn hungry on the midwatch below! So probably it was more an act of survival than a malicious theft I concluded that here was a chance to exercise real leadership!

I turned to the sailor and said, in a loud tone does that look like ladies' panties to you, sailor "NO SIR" came the sharp reply. Well, lock it up again I retorted and moved on to the next locker.

Strange thing, but every time I went down to the forward engine room, a sailor always appeared and asked me "how would you like to have a tuna fish sandwich, sir?" Don't mind if I do!

Years later, at a Goodrich reunion in Newport, R.I. I told this incident at the evening banquet festivities. When finished, I said "if that sailor is here tonight, I want him to come forward to the mike." No one appeared. But about 15 minutes after I sat down, two sailors came over to my table, and said "we were the ones!" I looked them in the eye and thought I recognized them. Then one sailor said "But you never knew about the other boxes we smuggled into the boiler room!"

Two years later, at the next Goodrich reunion, everyone took their places at the tables for the main banquet.

At each place setting was a small tin box of tuna fish, marked with a label: 'Compliments of the Chief Engineer, Mr. Bosshardt !'

Our first port of call was in Naples, Italy. When the ship tied up, there was always a flurry of activity, with the usual visitors and services coming aboard, and a rush to post the liberty list for the sailors going ashore that night. Most of this administrative work was carried on by the Executive officer, Mr. Wrocklage. I knew that in this particular Port we would not be taking on water from the dock, but manufacturing our own water. Therefore the question came up about the quantity of chlorine I should use to purify the water coming out of the bay. It was the first time I had this problem as Chief Engineer, so I asked Mr. Wrocklage for his guidance. But Mr. Wrocklage was totally stressed out making decisions right and left with the flurry of activity, and he explained in a loud tone "MAX, there are 800,000 people in the city of Naples. Just assume that they take a shit twice a day and you can damn well figure out yourself how much chlorine to use" and with that he stormed off.

During the midshipmen training cruise, we had midshipmen attached to every department and activity to receive training. This was certainly an extra burden besides standing watch and conducting our own departmental work. I guess one night, on the midwatch, from 00:00 to 04:00 h, when Leo was O.O.D. and I was his J.O.O.D, it reached the point when some humor was needed. We had a first-class midshipmen (senior) on the helm steering the ship. He was a particularly obnoxious person, who thought he knew it all. So Leo surreptitiously turned off the selsyn transmitter which transmits the position of the steering wheel back to after steering compartment to control the rudder. Of course, the ship started drifting off course and no matter what the midshipman did, he could not get it back on course. About that time, Leo looked over his shoulder and said "you are not on course, get back on course". Then in a loud voice Leo exclaimed "Bridge has lost steering control!" By this time the midshipman was thoroughly shaken and in a sweat. Leo turned the transmitter back on, and let him steer us back to our base course. Knowledge of the port and starboard selsyn transmitters was not well known among most of the ship's officers and crew. And that was true of our captain as well, as I will describe later in this book. An incident occurred which nearly caused a serious collision.

Leo was in charge of the electronics department, and his dozen or so sailors under him were designated as ET's, or electronic technicians. They were perhaps the sharpest

and most intelligent sailors on the ship. One of his men was named Ivan, who was a short, dumpy jewish boy with orange hair! Ivan was an expert on the electronic gear and knew it inside out. But socially, he was a bit of a nerd.

It was on the occasion of our return from the Med Cruise, as we arrived at our homeport of Newport Rhode Island. Ivan approached Leo, because not only was Leo head of the Electronics Department, but also acted as the division officer tending to the personal needs of his men. Ivan told Leo that he had noticed an attractive lady coming in a convertible to pick him up when he went on shore. He wanted to know if that was his wife. Leo answered in the affirmative, and asked him why he wanted to know. Ivan asked if he had children, and Leo said that they had none but would like some. Then Ivan said you are the right person for me to ask an important question. Tonight I am meeting a girl for a first date. I need to know how to keep her out of trouble, meaning that he didn't want to make her pregnant. With an absolutely straight face Leo told Ivan, do you have any idea why your testicles hang outside your body? No Sir replied Ivan. Leo continued, it is because the body temperature is too high and will kill the sperm. So I suggest to you that when that magic moment arrives, you excuse yourself, go to the bathroom, draw a basin full of lukewarm water, and dip your testicles in the water for 20 minutes. That will kill the sperm, And your girlfriend will be perfectly safe. Ivan thanked him profusely.

The next morning, at quarters, there was no sign of Ivan. Leo was concerned and went to sick bay where he found Ivan. What happened he asked Ivan. Ivan said that when that magic moment arrive, he was so excited, that he drew a basin of extremely hot water and thought that submerging his testicles for only 10 minutes would do the same thing. And now, explained Ivan, I can't walk!

On August 29, 1954, I had planned to marry Joan Clifton,

whom I had dated at Cornell University. So I requested leave of about two weeks for the wedding and honeymoon. Prior to departing the ship, and after requesting the leave, every day in the wardroom during meal time, the captain kept telling me it was not possible for me to miss the ship's operations, which had been scheduled to go to Little Creek, Virginia for amphibious landings. He suggested I get a hotel room for Joan nearby, and it might be possible for me to stay on shore one or two nights. At that point I had not yet been promoted to LT (jg) nor had I become Chief Engineer. I was still a partly gullible Ensign. Of course, this worried me immensely as the time approached for me to leave.

I had, indeed, been informed I could go. But we had selected a fancy hotel in Portsmouth, New Hampshire for our honeymoon. Then I took a beating from the other officers who pointed out that Portsmouth was the location of a naval prison, and my honeymoon was only a cover-up!

Of course, I drove my car with my new bride to Portsmouth. As it turned out, hurricane Carol moved up the coast at the same time. During the ship's absence the pier in Newport was inundated with about five feet of seawater and totally ruined all the cars parked there. When the hurricane hit Portsmouth, the hotel lost power, but was able to cook on gas stoves. They issued hurricane lanterns to the guests to find their way to their rooms. Many of the small boats in the harbor ended up on the front lawn of the hotel. But the hotel made the best of it, and brought in a hypnotist for a demonstration one evening in candlelight while the wind was howling outside.

CHAPTER 9

Life Under The New Captain

After returning from Europe to our homeport, in Newport Rhode Island, we were engaged during the fall and winter of 1954 in various operations with units of the Atlantic Fleet.

About this time CDR Thomas Keegan was relieved by CDR John Neff as the ship's captain. He was a short, feisty man. When he got angry, sometimes over inconsequential details, we used to say he would "vibrate". He was a stickler for correct protocol. He almost bordered on a "Captain Queeg" personality.

An example of this was the occasion when the mess deck called up to the bridge to request permission to secure the chow line. This was done in order to make sure all men on watch ha been relieved to go eat. On this particular day there was a brand new seaman apprentice on the bridge telephone. Receiving the request, instead of going to the Officer of the Deck, he went to the captain and said "Sir, they wish to secure the chow line". The captain, wishing to have communications conducted properly, said in a loud voice "who are they?". The sailor stepped back, spoke again over the sound powered telephone to the mess deck, and then came back to the captain and said "they didn't say, sir" The captain, at that point, blew his stack!

Referring back to the question of commanding officers and their familiarity with technical questions concerning the ships propulsion plant, such an incident did occur at this time. The *Goodrich* was operating with a task unit of ships, and it was steaming alongside an aircraft carrier in order to refuel. Refueling for destroyers occurred about every third day underway, because they had to remain at least at 80 percent or more fueled in case of emergencies. Thus, the *Goodrich* was close on the starboard side of the carrier matching its speed precisely, and connected to the carrier with four large size oil hoses taking on fuel. I happened to be standing on the main deck observing, when through the ships loudspeakers I heard "bridge has lost steering control". The captain took over the con, ordered the port engine stopped, the starboard engine full astern, and all fuel hoses jettisoned. In those few seconds of no steering control, the heavy hoses began drawing the *Goodrich* toward the carrier. I have to complement Captain Neff's quick thinking, which slowed the *Goodrich*, and going astern on the starboard screw forced the bow away from the carrier. By a very close margin, we slipped under the stern of the carrier. Oil sprayed everywhere.

The next thing I heard over the loudspeaker was "now the Chief Engineer report to the bridge immediately". When I got to the bridge, Captain Neff leaped at me, and grabbed my throat pinning me against the bulkhead shouting "what have you done to me Max?" This was the moment when my superior knowledge of the propulsion plant would save my ass. I explained to the captain that two Selsyn transmitters on the bridge connect with a hydraulic control lever in the after steering compartment. It would have only been necessary for someone on the bridge to switch from one selsyn to the other to regain steering control in seconds. Even failing that, the bridge telephone talker could tell the sailor on watch in after steering to steer a certain course, since he had a compass repeater back there. It took no effort for him to move a small lever to control the hydraulic pistons, which in turn moved the rudders.

But in desperate ignorance, the captain had ordered the Gunnery Officer to take a boatswains mate and some sailors back to after steering, and prepare to rig a heavy block and tackle in order to move the two massive heavy rudders manually. This was not only physically practically impossible, but ludicrous as well.

However, the captain quickly understood and accepted what I told him and ordered me to hold school on all officers and men standing bridge watch, as well as all the sailors who stood watch in the after steering room.

Steaming with an aircraft carrier was one of our primary duties. Two destroyers would escort the carrier and perform plane guard duty. This means that one destroyer would follow the carrier by 1000 yards, and 15 degrees off dead astern. The other destroyer would steam 3000 yards off the port beam of the carrier. This was the orientation when steaming on a launch or recovery of aircraft operations into the wind. An aircraft about to land would fly over the destroyer 3000 yards to the left of the carrier, but in the opposite direction, and then commence a 'U' turn, banking to the left so that he could see the landing signal officer and his flags showing the pilot if he should adjust and come more left or right as he landed. Unfortunately, carrier landings and takeoffs are very hazardous, and on the average, we lost a plane into the water every week. Typically when a fighter plane ditched at sea, it would sink in about four minutes. So rescuing the pilot was of upmost urgency. If the weather was good, the carrier would also have a helicopter airborne which could reach the pilot quickly. But in foul weather, or at night, it was up to one of the destroyers to go full astern and stop to pick up the pilot. The destroyer following astern of the carrier would reach a pilot who had ditched astern of the carrier because he came in too low. Sometimes, if there was a miss-firing of the catapult launch mechanism on the carrier, or the wrong one fired, a plane would be thrown into the water off the bow. In one instance, at night, a plane attempted to land and flew over the flight deck too high, missed all the arresting cable's, flew into the cable crash barrier, causing it to break, and he went over the bow into the sea. Unfortunately, when the cables split it lashed out sidewards and killed seven sailors on deck. The destroyer on the left side of the carrier was able to back down quickly, put their whaleboat into the water, and located the pilot who had a small flashing light on his lifejacket. Because of the traumatic shock of crashing, they were ordered not to inform him of the deaths of the sailors on the carrier until the next day.

In the event we had picked up a pilot, we would then

steam along side the carrier the next day, and rig a high-line over to the carrier. As a reward for saving the pilot, the carrier would normally send over a large container of cake for the crew. But on the next occasion, if the supply department failed to get the empty container up on deck and ready to return it, there was real hell coming from Captain Neff.

That was just one of his peculiarities He always ordered the junior ensign, in our case, George Crawford (from the Naval Academy) to go down to sample the cruise mess, and report back to the captain that the food was satisfactory. The captain always insisted on having Frank's red hot pepper sauce at this time served on our table as well.

The officer who was head of the Supply Department, and I, as Chief Engineer, had a pact between us. Every once in a while George would report that the garbage grinder on the mess deck was inoperative. If the captain confronted me, I would tell him that the messcooks had dropped another piece of silverware in the garbage grinder causing it to jam. If the captain confronted the supply officer first, he would always say that they informed ny electricians, who had not shown up to fix the problem!

At the end of our two weeks training in Guantánamo, we

were at anchor in the bay. The captain had been called to a meeting at a location near the entrance to the bay. That day I was command duty officer on board. At about mid-day, we received a message from the captain that I was to get the ship underway at 1500 h. and steam to the entrance of the bay, where he would come out on a launch to board the ship.

Of course, this was very exciting because it was the first time I would actually command the ship underway. As Chief Engineer, it was no problem for me to give orders to the main engine room to warm up the main plant and be ready to get underway at 1500 h. The warm up takes two hours. But as far as giving orders via the bridge telephone talker to the boatswains mate's on the bow, regarding the anchor, I was at a total loss. So I sent word down to have the Gunnery Officer, Silas Keehn, come up to the bridge immediately. I told him to stand next to me and whisper the proper commands, which I then relayed down to the sailors at the bow in order to hoist anchor!

At that point it was quite a thrill to give the orders to proceed at 1/3 speed, turn the ship around and proceed on a course to take us to the rendezvous point at the entrance to the bay, where we stopped and picked up the captain.

Upon completing our annual training in Guantamamo, we were steaming alone in a relaxed manner back to our home base in Newport Rhode Island. It was a sunny quiet Sunday afternoon, somewhere along the Florida coast, when the Executive Officer, Mr. Wrocklage, happened to be strolling on the main deck aft. Suddenly he saw an oil slick leaving the ship. Of course, I was ordered to make an immediate inspection below and determine what was happening. I called my Chief Boiler Tender, Taylor, to my stateroom. He brought with him the BT first class, Smith, who is designated as the ships Oil King. They had already discovered the problem, which was in a ship's cross connection line valve, used to trim up the oil tanks port and starboard. In making some repairs, he had mistakenly left a rag in the gate valve preventing it from closing completely. As a result, oil had been flowing through the line and out into an overboard excess spell line. After taking a total of the oil tank level gauges, it was determined that we had already lost some 10,000 gallons of oil over the side!

It was a serious error. But the Oil king was an extremely reliable person, hard worker, and had been studying hard to prepare for his examination for promotion to Chief BT. Reporting this incident would surely have cost him his chances to become chief. Later, in discussion with Chief

Taylor, we agreed that for the sake of good leadership and desire not to ruin a good man's career, we would concoct another reason for the loss of oil, and the real reason would remain secret among the three of us. So I reported to the captain that the crossover valve had broken and was not functioning properly as the cause for the leakage. Later our Oil King passed examination for chief, and it was probably the most expensive promotion the Navy has had!

During our Mediterranean cruise of 1954 - 1955, my new wife and I experienced being alone and separated for four months. Much lovesick separation causes one to do extreme things. For example, sometimes I would stand watch in CIC (combat information center) where we had all our radar equipment and planting tables. But when we were steaming alone, there was virtually nothing for the CIC officer to do during his four hour watch. So I would locate our ships position on the globe, and determine in which compass direction, and what depression angle under the horizon I would have to cast my gaze, in order to look directly at the spot where my new bride was waiting in Newport Rhode Island.

Being newlyweds, we wrote each other a letter every evening, and being lovesick as we were, they contained very gooey content. Actually, being at sea most of the time, we only entered a port about once a week or less often. Each time we did so there was a stack of mail waiting for me from my new bride. Even though I was Chief Engineer by that time, and had my own state room, it was filled to the brim with classified documents, instruction books, voice tubes, telephones, and bubble level showing the trim of the ship, And nowhere to store all these letters except in among my clothes. In the 50s, it was common practice that the black sailors normally served in the supply department, and some acted as stewards, taking care of the officer state rooms, their bedding and their laundry. What to do with the letters became a real problem because if any ever found their way among the crew, I would be the laughing stock of the ship.

I lived in after officers quarters on the main deck. One of my fellow officers suggested that I wait for a stormy night, tie up the letters in bundles, and throw them over the side. I thought that was the best solution. In the next days we did enter a very severe storm, and after dark, I went out on the main deck with several bundles of letters held together with rubber bands. The sea and the wind were so wild I had no idea which way it was blowing. I heaved the first bundle into the air over the water, and to my horror the rubber band broke in mid air and all the letters blue back on board the ship! Being wet, they naturally stuck everywhere, on deck and even on the gun mounts. I had to get up at five the next morning and at daybreak went out and peeled every single letter from its sticking point. I do believe that none of the letters were ever read by anyone else. Of course, in my very next letter to my wife I emphatically stated DON'T SEND ANY MORE LETTERS!

CHAPTER 10

My Final Meditteranean Cruise

The *Goodrich* was assigned to the Mediterranean Sixth Fleet again during the winter of 1955–1956. By this time, my wife was a seasoned navy wife. So she, and Marcia Keehn, wife of the Gunnery Officer, and Lorraine Peterson, wife of our squadron's medical doctor, dreamed up a plan to follow our ship around the Mediterranean. Our normal itinerary consisted of operating with the carrier task unit during one week, then moor each time at a different Mediterranean Port the second week, and then repeating the cycle. This meant that the wives would have to determine each week where the next port was going to be, and travel there arriving before we arrived. Their normal source of information was at the American Consulate in the particular country to which we would next travel. Typically there could be several ports in Italy, France, and Spain.

Our Executive Officer, Mr. Wrocklage, who was the ships navigator, told me he never had to find out at which dock we were supposed to moor, because he simply had to look through the binoculars and find three women, in a brown coat, a gray coat, and a red coat waiting for us!

In some ports we had to anchor out in the harbor. If I did not have the watch one night, I could have the captain's gig take me to the harbor pier, and I could enjoy the evening with my wife. Then they would pick me up the next morning in time to be on board at 08:00 h. Or if I have the watch, I would be permitted to bring her out to the ship for dinner in the officers wardroom, watch the movie, and then return her back to shore for the night.

The three wives had committed themselves to operate on a budget each of five dollars per day, not counting meals we would have together. Prior to our ship coming into Cannes, on the French Riviera, the three decided to book one room to save money. Then when the fleet appeared in the bay, they had to try to communicate with the landlady that now they wanted three double rooms as long as the fleet was there. They didn't speak any French and the landlady spoke no English. I am sure they realize that the landlady thought they were prostitutes praying on the Navy personnel! One room had a view on the bay with a bathroom, but only having a sink and bidet, but no toilet. The second bedroom was the only one with a double bed, but the window was over the kitchen and quite noisy The third bedroom had twin beds, and a full bathroom with bathtub. Taking into account the fact that at that time the hot water was being conserved, and only turned on in the mornings and evenings during high usage. So the ladies drew straws and each night we would switch bedrooms to take full advantage of each of the fine points of the particular rooms.

Near the end of our cruise, during the Christmas season, my wife, Joan, traveled to Switzerland to meet my mother. She was then introduced to all of our relatives in Switzerland. I was able to take several days leave and joined her there. With one cousin and his wife, we were introduced to fondue at the best restaurant in Zürich. We also took a trip to one of the best ski areas in Switzerland; Davos. We ascended on the Parsenn Bahn, and took the aerial cable car to the summit of Weissflujoch at 2,800 meters. However, without skiis we were the sole ludicrous passengers descending again on the cable car! But it was exhilarating.

After I departed to go back to my ship in Naples, Joan had booked a passage back to the US from Genoa, Italy to New York on the Andrea Doria. But upon my return to the ship, I learned that we were taking on fuel, provisions and ammunition, as we had been ordered to go into the Red Sea for one month, during the Suez crisis of 1956. The Egyptian dictator, Nassar, had threatened to close the Suez Canal, and the English and French governments threatened to invade Egypt if he did so. Although we were neutral, it was decided that in the case of closure we would have a naval vessel in the Red Sea as a precaution.

There is always something good that comes out of evil! As a result of our orders, I phoned my wife in Switzerland, and she decided to take the Andrea Doria only from Genoa to Naples, and disembark there, in order to say goodbye to me. Then she booked another ship for the rest of the trip home. That was divine providence. When the Andrea Doria was approaching New York off the coast of Cape Cod, early in the morning in a fog, a Swedish vessel, the Stockholm, was approaching from the opposite direction. According to the rules of the road the Stockholm came right in order to pass the Andrea Doria port to port. However, The Andrea Doria was behind schedule, and wanted to make a straight line course towards New York City, which meant they would have to come quite a bit left. Apparently the officer on watch was inexperienced. He did not notify his captain, nor did he signal the Stockholm that they were going to pass starboard to starboard, so the Stockholm kept coming further right to pass port to port. Eventually there was a collision, and some passengers on the Andrea Doria were killed. The crew of the Andrea Doria abandoned ship in the lifeboats, and left many passengers remaining on the ship, some of whom died in the next several days as the ship sank. The entire episode has been documented in a book called "Collision Course", and I understand that the Italian Line made a huge settlement out of court. Of course, my wife avoided that tragedy because of the Suez Crisis!

CHAPTER 11

The Suez Crisis

We departed Naples the next day, and steam directly to Port Said off the Egyptian coast.

There was a strange sense of urgency, as we heaved to in waters we have never visited. Another destroyer emerged from the Suez Canal which had already been stationed in the Red Sea. We managed to make a highline transfer and exchange movie films, one of which were shown every night on board ship.

We then steamed southwards through the northern half of the Suez Canal to Bitter Lake. Since the Canal can only accommodate the width of one ship, we had to rendez-vous with a northbound group of ships bypassing them in bitter lake. As we arrived first, we tied up to a pier on the western side of the lake. Unfortunately, a violence sandstorm came up from the west, which parted our mooring lines, and the ship was pushed over to the east side of the lake onto sand bars in shallow water. All ships remained in Bitter Lake until the storm subsided. Several boatswain's mates went in the gig and hauled a mooring line back over to the pier, and on the ship wound the line around a windless and attempted to pull the ship into deeper water. But the windless motor was unable to move the ship and burned up. At that point, the captain instructed me to go into the main engine room, to determine if one of our five blades on the porch propeller was stuck in the sand. I took a screwdriver, put it to my ear and rested the end of it on our main engine reduction gear casing. Then I ordered a machinist mate to engage the jacking gear. This was a small AC motor with a 100 to 1 reduction gear, that is used to turn over the main turbines slowly when first injecting steam, in order to warm up the turbans evenly. The second he engaged the motor I yelled stop, as I heard a horrible scraping sound as the propeller blade inched through the sand bar.

With no more wind blowing, we managed to use our starboard engine and full left rudder position, as there was a runner behind each propeller, to move the stern off the sandbar But as we got underway through the canal, and due to the shallow water in the canal, we knew we had a bench propeller blade because any attempt to exceed 13 knots resulted in a violent vibration of the port propeller shaft. Nevertheless, we were obliged to continue our trip into the Red Sea since there was no location where we could get major repairs until we were relieved to get out of the Red Sea again.

As we proceeded slowly to our first port, several noteworthy incidents occurred. First, an oil tanker owned by an American oil company was proceeding on its way back to the US through the Red Sea. The mate of the watch was delighted to see an American destroyer. He climbed up on the signal bridge, and flashed us a message in Morse cod telling us where he had come from, what his name was, and where he was heading, all the while passing us by. At the end of his message he asked "who are you?" But we were under wartime security measures, and we're only allowed to answer with our call sign, NBAN, or "nan baker able nan". As he steamed off into the distance, he sent a final flashing light message back: "fuck you". I can't blame him!

Next we encountered a ship passing from Egypt across the Red Sea to the Arabian Peninsula. On board deck we could see dozens of black women, who no doubt had been collected to be taken to the harems of the wealthy Arabs.

And then, a Russian Fraser passed us, but despite our challenging him with our international call sign, he made no reply.

Finally we arrived in our first port of call, Port Sudan, Sudan. My first job as Chief Engineer was to survey the dock area and record any shipyard facilities that I could see. This was all part of the war readiness. It was there that I first encountered the "Fuzzy Wuzzy's." These were the aborigine people of the Sudan, who had wild fuzzy hair all over their heads, with beards, and have the unusual habit of standing on one leg and resting their other leg around a walking stick. They were dockworkers, but looked rather ferocious with their small animal bones pierced through their noses.

Then a Mercedes pulled up to the gangway of our ship at the pier, and the Governor of Sudan paid an official call on the captain. The interesting part is that his two companions were a British Army and a British Naval officer as attaches. That was certainly a strong indication of what we had always heard, namely, that the British were the only occupiers of African colonies who gave them their independence in a totally organized fashion instead of plundering and departing.

That evening our ship played host to a large group of

Sudanese men and women dressed in very colorful attire. Our ship was rigged with flags and lighting, music playing, and the ship's officers we're obliges to dance with the Sudanese women. This was made more difficult by the fact that we wore our heavily starched dress white uniforms complete with a sword, which made dancing, and sitting down very difficult! It was the only time during my entire service that I wore the white dress uniform.

We limped across the Red Sea to our next port of call in Jedda, Saudi Arabia. Then we encountered another set of circumstances. Women were not seen in public unless totally covered and escorted by a family member. They were not allowed to drive a car. In the best hotels one could not buy an alcoholic drink. One could only drink a horrible kind of tea in the lobby. Furthermore, if they had a swimming pool, one day was for the men, and a different day for women. In the hotels, the TV broadcast only one station, controlled by the government and mainly propaganda.

Our ship's crew were permitted to go on liberty, but had to be back on board by sundown. The result was that black market alcohol was bootlegged and sold to the crew over the ship's rail from the pier at the stern of the ship and out of sight. It was a very hot climate, and in no

time the crew on board got very drunk drinking the alcohol. This all became known when two sailors decided
to see who could cut a longer slice down the other guys
arm. Eventually one sailor's artery got cut and he had to
be rushed to the hospital!

One evening, I had the shore patrol duty, and rode around
town in a jeep with a sailor driving. Of course, there was
nothing to do because all crew members were on board
ship. So we decided to drive out of town and proceed
down the road to Mecca. Well, we had only gone a mile
or two before we encountered an Army Post and barrier.
We were questioned as to whether we were Christians,
and therefore infidels. And so we were barred from proceeding any further.

On one of the days in port, the captain and the executive
officer departed to pay a call on the American Consul
General in Jedda. It was my turn to be Command Duty
Officer in charge of the ship while in port. So we decided
to arrange for an open house for the Saudis to visit on
board. We rigged lines along the main deck, around the
gun mounts, up on the bridge, and down into main control
engine room. Hundreds of Saudis showed up; all young
men and no women. About noon a sailor ran up to me
and said "Mr. Bosshardt, they are all going down into the

main engine room but no one is coming out!" My God, I thought, now what in the hell is going on down there? So I personally went below to the main engine room and discovered that a sailor had forgotten to remove a large calendar picture on the bulkhead of Marylyn Munroe completely naked! It was the sensation of the day.

One has to wonder what the deal is when American and European engineers, with their technology, went to Saudi Arabia and helped the desert Bedouins at the time bring all that oil to the surface And yet, we still have to buy the oil at the prevailing market price. The answer became evident, when I had a chance to go ashore and was invited by the local American Arabian Oil company executive to visit his home. Privately, of course, he served all the liquor we could drink. He explained that he was on a two year assignment, that his beautiful quarters and expenses were all paid for on an expense account, and his very high salary was directly deposited in a bank account in New York. Every second year he had two months vacation back in the US. He explained that he went a bit wild spending so much money on his vacation, that he had to return for an additional two year contract because he was broke!

One other incident was told to me by Dick Beyers, Radarman First Class.

"We went out to the ARAMCO compound to play a game of softball. Afterwards we were entertained in one of their homes with refreshments. Much like the Consul General, these folks had their own still and each month it was rotated through the compound. They made some pretty powerful stuff. I don't recall what the ingredients were, but it was pretty potent. Needless to say when we returned to the ship some of us were just a bit tipsy."

CHAPTER 12

The Eventful Trip Home

Dictator Nasser backed down, did not close the Suez Canal, and the British and the French never had to invade Egypt. So the *Goodrich* was relieved of its assignment in the Red Sea.

We limped through the Suez Canal and across the length of the Mediterranean at 13 nuts. Making arrangements with the British Navy, we were able to enter the British naval ship yard at Gibraltar, and go into drydock. To be sure, one of our five blades of the propeller, which in total had a diameter of some 12 feet, and was severely bent. The propeller had to be removed. The docking officer passed the word up in a loud booming voice, that we were to lower the propeller nut wrench. As Chief Engineer, when taking over my duties, I had to sign about 200 Title 'B' cards, each of which listed any piece of equipment belonging to the engineering department that was not a fixed part of the installation. So I knew there was a large wrench, open ended, and about 8 feet long, that was bolted to the ship structure aft. It took several sailors to unbolt the wrench, and lift it onto a shipyard crane. It was then lowered down into drydock. Very shortly thereafter, I heard the docking officer shout up in an angry tone "this is no propeller nut wrench, it's a god-damn rudder post'wrench! " With great embarrassment I had to ask the chief engineer of our sistership, which was in Gibraltor with us, if I could borrow his propeller nut wrench. God knows what happened to ours!

To make the embarrassment worse, he happened to be a graduate of the Merchant Marine Academy, and we always were trading jibes about the Navy versus the Merchant Marine.

Our propeller was laid on a flat surface, and the blade was wrapped with induction heating cables and heated up to a high temperature. And then a shipyard worker actually stood up on that table with a sledgehammer and pounded our bronze propeller blade back to its original shape!

That same morning, several of us not on duty were invited to visit a British frigate at the next pier. As we entered the wardroom, a steward came up immediately and asked "would you like to have a scotch, sir?". I was amazed that officers were allowed to drink on a working day, and learned that the crew also were served a ration of rum every day. I politely asked if it would be possible for me to transfer to the British Navy?

We then were able to proceed at normal cruising speed's across the Atlantic to our homeport in Newport, Rhode Island. But since we were steaming alone, there was no chance to refuel underway. As a result, we approached Cape Cod with only 20% fuel left on board. At that point, we received a radio message that a huge storm was approaching from the north west at almost hurricane force. In those days, ships still had to moor at large metal buoys in the bay of Newport. If the weather was bad enough, the crew were not able to go ashore in the liberty boat. Our ship was, therefore, ordered to remain at see until the storm had passed. Because our oil tanks were already 80% empty, the captain called me to the bridge, and expressed concern over the fact that we were rolling heavily in the waves building up in the storm. He wanted me to stabilize the ship by taking on sea water into the oil tanks. I explained to the captain that because seawater was heavier than oil, it would lay at the bottom of the tanks, pushing the sludge and oil higher in the tanks. Because we took the oil from the tanks through standpipes about 8 inches high off the bottom of the tank to feed the boilers, the sea water would remain at the level of the top of the standpipes It could occur that at some point the sea water would be fed to the burners in the boilers, putting out the fires and losing propulsion. But the captain preferred to have a stable ship for the night and take his chances with the see water.

Although I was serving my last two months on board the ship, due to be retired from active duty, I was still very nervous about the captain's request. If we ever took sea water in the burners and lost propulsion power it could result in a serious collision. And then I, and my BT's, might be easily blamed for causing the situation. Therefore, I made a very unpopular decision and asked the captain to give me the order in writing to ballast the oil tanks with sea water. As expected, he was very angry about it, but I did get his order in writing.

CHAPTER 13

Collision On The Elbe River

After I left the ship, the *Goodrich* proceeded back to Europe. The following is an account provided by my shipmate, LT (jg) Bob Perry, who was still on board:

"On July 1956 *USS Goodrich (DDR-831)* and a Dutch freighter collided in the fog at 0355 in the morning on the Elbe River, Germany.

After returning from a seven month Med cruise in March of 1956, the *Goodrich* was selected to go on a six week midshipman cruise that summer.

For the Midshipman Cruise, two great Northern European ports were on our list of cities that we were scheduled to visit: Gothenburg, Sweden, followed by Hamburg, Germany and then a quick stop in GTMO before we returned to Newport. We were in Sweden during the Summer Solstice or as they call it Midsummer's Eve; a week long holiday and for most Swedes probably the most important holiday of the year. During our visit the Midshipmen, as well as our own ship's company had a great time and attended a number of events celebrating the longest day of the year. Old fashioned drinking songs are an important part of this feast so we were all happy to oblige and join the locals in their celebration.

After a memorable visit to Gothenburg, we headed on a southerly course through the North Sea to the mouth of the Elbe River and then headed southeast toward Hamburg, 60 miles up the river. It was now July, but the weather was cold, rainy and foggy. We were steaming at a fairly fast speed (up to 20 knots), considering the reduced visibility and overall bad weather. *Goodrich* was in company of a heavy cruiser, USS Des Moines (CA-134) and one other Destroyer, the USS Vesole (DDR-878). Des Moines was carrying an Admiral as the Task Unit Commander. Steaming in a column formation up the Elbe River, the Three ship unit was scheduled to arrive in Hamburg in the morning of the 4th of July, so the Admiral was keeping the speed up in spite of the fog, to forestall a late arrival.

I was scheduled to be the OOD on the 0400 to 0800

watch that morning. Because of the horrible weather, I was dressed in foul weather gear. When I arrived on the bridge the exec told me that we had picked up speed during the mid-watch and we would be reaching Hamburg before 0800 and that he wanted me in dress Blues. So I went below to after officers quarters and quickly changed into my Blues. I arrived on the bridge a few minutes later and said to LT (jg) George Crawford, "I am ready to relieve you". George quickly responded "we better wait, things don't look good ahead". We had an Elbe River Pilot on board who was helping our Navigator (the exec) guide us through the dark and foggy river.

A few seconds later, I heard the River Pilot yell out through a bull horn ro the freighter, "Go ahead, you crazy bastard!".

This is what had happened ...a Dutch freighter had decided to anchor in the river because of the poor visibility. After dropping its hook, the freighter backed down to set the anchor in the Elbe River muddy bottom. During this backing down movement, the freighter was blocking our path to pass astern of the freighter, and it caught the *Goodrich* on its port side and raked everything clean including our motor whaleboat boat and its davits as well as a dual 3 inch 50 mount on the 01 level port side. All our damage was above the waterline so we were still seaworthy, but the ship's appearance was not pretty. To add insult to injury, we had bounced off the freighter and ended up on the bank of the Elbe River aground in the mud. Upon a complete assessment of our hull damage, we were able to free ourselves fairly quickly from the mud bank by reversing our engines and then proceeded to Hamburg. After spending a few days in Hamburg, we sailed back down the Elbe River and steamed to the German Navy yard at Bremerhaven, where they cleaned up our damaged area and made us "Ready for Sea" in less than a week. The German shipyard workers did a wonderful job including creating their own formula of haze grey paint for the entire port side from stem to stern.

After repairs at Bremerhaven, we joined the rest of the Midshipman cruise ships at sea and proceeded across the Atlantic to GTMO. It wasn't until we arrived at GTMO and tried to do some antisubmarine work that we discovered our sonar dome was damaged in the grounding.

Another bit of irony, the motor whale boat that got "totaled" in the collision did not belong to the *Goodrich*. We had borrowed it from the cruiser, Des Moines a week or so earlier while we were in Gothenburg because we had an engine failure with our own motor whaleboat.

As it turns out, fate was kind to me. Arriving on the bridge in the wrong uniform saved my naval career of 26 years. If I had relieved George Crawford, I would have been at the Con during the collision. George, a Naval Academy grad, resigned his commission a few years after the incident. The captain and the exec both had successful careers and retired at the rank of Captains. A Board of Inquiry headed by the Admiral on board the Des Moines found the *Goodrich* at no fault in the collision.

CHAPTER 14

The Bottom Line

This narrative describes many humorous incidents, as well as tragic mistakes which quite often were very dangerous situations. However, in looking back over my time on board the *USS Goodrich DDR 831*, I must draw the proper conclusion.

First of all, I am extremely proud to have served in the U.S. Navy particularly at a time when the Korean War was in progress, the Suez Crisis occurred, we had confrontations with stalking Russian submarines, and we were continuously in a rescue mode during carrier flight operations which often resulted in serious accidents.

I also credit the U.S. Navy with a superior combination of onboard training, excellent training schools, and the progression of responsibilities at a young age, which I would never have experienced in civilian corporate life.

So I complement my fellow officers and sailors on the ship, and especially the 90 men under me in the Engineering Department, who gave me such excellent cooperation. This was demonstrated in their superior skills in maintaining our engineering plant.

Today, in a time when values and standards have crumbled to such a low level, and with such lack of respect and discipline, it would behoove a young person not in school or college to consider serving in the military. He would regain his sense of respect and discipline as well as have the opportunity to attend excellent schools and learn a profession or skill.

CPSIA information can be obtained
at www.ICGtesting.com
Printed in the USA
LVHW050305170821
695470LV00009B/789

9 781977 232151